Looking S.E. Front Door in Forecourt

Elevation 1: 100

View 2   Forecourt and
          Main Front

View 1   Courtyard with Cloister passage
          connecting front and back block

AN ARCHITECT'S SKETCHBOOK

NICHOLAS JOHNSTON: DESIGNS, DRAWINGS AND BUILDINGS

ROSIE JOHNSTON
PHOTOGRAPHS BY CHRISTOPHER SYKES

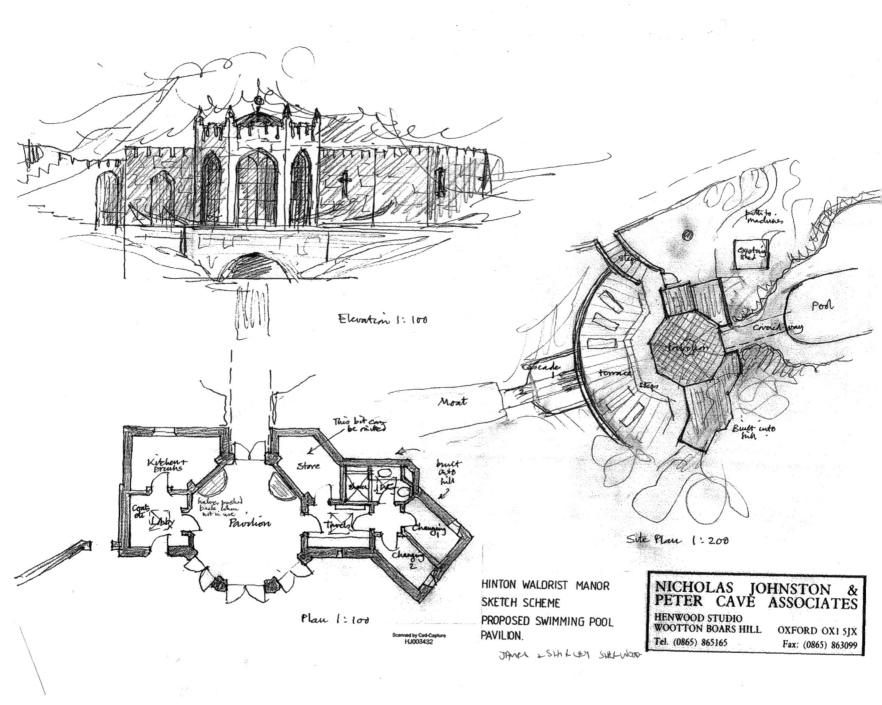

Elevation 1: 100

This bit can be minted

Store

built into hill

Kitchen + drains

halves pushed back when not in use

Coats etc Lobby

Pavilion

Shower WC

Towels

Changing 1

Changing 2

Plan 1: 100

path to meadows

Existing shed

Pool

Covered way

Pavilion

Cascade

terrace

step

Built into hill

Moat

Site Plan 1: 200

HINTON WALDRIST MANOR
SKETCH SCHEME
PROPOSED SWIMMING POOL
PAVILION.

JAMES & SHIRLEY SHELWOOD

NICHOLAS JOHNSTON &
PETER CAVE ASSOCIATES
HENWOOD STUDIO
WOOTTON BOARS HILL   OXFORD OX1 5JX
Tel. (0865) 865165   Fax: (0865) 863099

CONTENTS

ACKNOWLEDGEMENTS

A huge, extended thank you to:

Peter Cave
Everyone at Henwood Studios, past
and present

Clients NJJ has worked for (over and above those featured in the book):
Sarah Alexander
Nicholas and Diana Baring
Robin and Anne Baring
Belinda Belville and David Whately
Mark and Arabella Boxer
Michael and Isabel Briggs
Joanna Burne
Lindsay and Sarah Bury
Ian and Mary Cameron
Anthea and Jeremy Carver
Charles Cayzer
Colette Clark
William and Caroline Courtauld
Nell Dunn
Philip and Domenica Dunne
Anne Egerton
Simon and Annabel Elliot
Harry and Anna Erne
Bill and Carol Fox
Kim Fraser and Joanna Fraser
Simon and Jenny Fraser
Lucian Freud

Christopher Gibbs
Clive and Anne Gibson
Anne Glenconner
Judy and Michael Green
Robin and Rupert Hambro
Robert Heber Percy
Drue Heinz
Tanya and Anthony Hobson
John and Caryl Hubbard
Martin and Evelyn Jacomb
Zanie and Peter Jamieson
Mary Keen
TRH The Duke and Duchess of Kent
Amabel Lindsay
Laura Lindsay
Rupert and Josephine Loewenstein
Anthony and Jenny Loehnis
Christopher Loyd
Tony and Sophy Lund
Candida and Rupert Lycett Green
George and Diana Melly
David Mlinaric
Cecilia McEwen
Gilly Morris
Willy Mostyn Owen
David and Carolyn Newbigging
John Julius and Mollie Norwich
Nick and Suki Paravacini
Robin and Jennifer Plunket
Lily Pollock

Arthur and Madeleine Ponsonby
David and Mary Russell
Simon Sainsbury
Bruce Shand
Jeremy and Susanna Soames
Anthony and Penny Spink
James and Alyson Spooner
John Stefanidis
Isobel Strathmore
Elizabeth Sutherland
Rosemary and Anthony Tennant
Christopher and Antonia Thynne
Roger and Carolyn Waters
Robert and Nicky Wilson
David Windsor-Clive
Philip and Catriona Wroughton

Those he has worked with:
Cathy Agnew
Yves Allier
Michael Balston
Charles Bosher
Campbells of Wantage
Jim Cowey
Bobby Dickson
Norma Elloway
Paul Errington
Bert Faulkner
Hugh Henry
Holloway White Allom Ltd

Chester Jones
Christopher King
Amabel Lindsay
Jessie Mills
Paul Naylor
Wendy Nicholls
David Osborne
Palmers of Tetbury
Graham Porcher and all at St Giles Joinery
Trevor Rich
JG Smith
Smiths Gore, Dumfries
Mike Spiers
Brian Stevens
Tom Stuart-Smith
Swallow and Pearson
Sue Terry
Sally Thompson
Ben Tindall and his office
Treasure and Son of Ludlow
Lucy Ward
Waughs of Dumfries
Joanna Wood
Elizabeth Wyndham
Melissa Wyndham
Trevor Yorke
Victoria Yorke

Christopher Sykes and I would like to thank:
David Allison
Laszlo Almasi
Peter Browne

Jacquie Cox
Sarah Kate Edwards
Les and Judy Gilmer
Mark Jones
Philip Shewan
Andrew Smith
Sofka Zinovieff

Nicholas Johnston for giving in.
Susanna Johnston for her support.
Clara Weatherall for her vision
and perseverance.

Christopher and I would also like to thank
all the owners of the houses who answered
questions, pulled out sketches and plans,
showed us round, gave us endless cups of
tea and delicious lunches, moved cars, lifted
furniture and lit fires. Their support and
enthusiasm for this book not only made it
possible but enormous fun.

My thanks to Christopher Sykes for his
wonderful photographs and for being
easy and accommodating at every turn.
Thank you to the astonishingly unflappable
Vanessa Green at The Urban Ant for her
beautiful design and layout.

Further thanks to Peter Cave, Moira Claydon
and everyone at JCA who helped with
archive material, chronology and contacts.

Notes on the text and photographs:
Where clients are quoted, I have used their
names in the first instance of speech or
dialogue and then their initials and a dash in
ensuing quotes.
In various instances we have used
photographs that were not taken by
Christopher Sykes. Some houses have been
sold on, as in the case of East Woodhay
and Donne Place. We could not get access
to photograph East Woodhay, so we used
the Knight, Frank brochure photographs.
Despite the Gilmers' generous offer to let
us photograph Donne Place, the interiors
had changed from Clive Sinclair's day so
we elected to use photographs taken at the
time. In both cases the photographs are low
resolution and could not be reproduced to a
high standard. Before photographs, as used
in Daneway, Rooksnest and Holland Farm,
belong to the owners.

A number of jobs were not included in
this book. Some owners wished to retain
complete privacy; others have moved or
died or the house has vanished, as in the
case of Lyall Mews.

Many of NJJ's sketches, drawn on the
back of envelopes and napkins, have also
disappeared. One of the aims of this book
was to gather what remains in one place.

FOREWORD
Christopher Gibbs

Nicky is subtle, sensitive, gentle, wise. He knows the architecture of these islands from the grand to the modest; he is attuned to the spirit and bones of our vernacular traditions. Nicky understands buildings, how to refresh and rearrange them to suit the needs of the client and of our times. He listens, he absorbs, he reflects. He is alert to the layers of construction that an old house reveals, to the language of mouldings and the materials used. He knows what to encourage or discourage, what the planning officer may allow, how to get round the planning officer when he won't allow, how to get the best out of the house, how to gently temper the client's wilder aspirations.

I've worked with Nicky for myself, for family, for friends and clients, on projects great and small. I know the immense skill and understanding he brings to the work at hand. His lightness of touch, firmness of purpose, warmth, enthusiasm, courtesy and wonderful humour are all add-ons to the knowledge and vision that make working with him such a pleasure.

It was 50 years ago that we worked together on Stargroves, a big Victorian house below the Berkshire downs, the recent purchase of a young Mick Jagger. I was the go-between and the producer of furniture and fireplaces that needed replacing. Nicky and I would drive together (I hadn't passed my test), stopping for breakfast on the way at a greasy-spoon café run by identical twins. The house had seen few changes since its servant days; there was still a system in the butler's pantry for collecting rainwater for the gentleman's shaving. Mick would come to survey the progress of the building, happily checking out a long-overdue transformation.

In the 1970s, Nicky helped me to reshape Davington Priory, a Kentish house of medieval origins knit to a Norman church. There was still an arm of cloister and much inspired and scholarly 19th-century reuse of medieval tiles and stained glass, and its later echoes, still in the old spirit. We opened up choked spaces, revealed lost vistas, plumbed and sparked and repainted scarlet strapwork and uplifting texts on the Kentish weatherboarding.

Our longest spell of work together was the resurrection of the Wormsley estate for Paul Getty. This secret kingdom had slumbered for a century or two and required over a decade of detailed and complex reordering. There were countless meetings with agents, lawyers, accountants, craftsmen and building experts in arcane skills. Our client, my old friend, came and looked after four years (though taking a lively interest throughout from his London eyrie) and went home delighted. It became the happiest of settings for the last and ripest ten years of his life and continues as the family home of his son, and a haven for his three passions, opera, cricket and bibliomania.

Looking at the long list of works by Nicky and his firm, I marvel at the variety of projects they've handled. Many are the fruits of long friendships or the milieu in which Nicky and Susanna move. They're almost all for individuals rather than faceless corporations or public bodies. Chiefly, he's worked on country houses great and small, pruning, paring, editing the unwieldy, pointing up former glories, removing the wilder anachronisms, conjuring harmony and grace out of muddle, make-do and mar.

Nicky's catalogue of projects, some of which have been lost in the mists of time, make a fascinating study. There are a few mammoth endeavours that have needed sustained teamwork; Wormsley and Glympton continued over many years. There are small works to local churches, quinquennial reports to be acted upon when the money could be found. Nicky and his partner Peter Cave have tamed and tuned many a London house and have built, modified and beautified houses in the far-flung corners of the world. Their practice's clients include the full spectrum of grandees: princes from Saudi

Arabia, our prime minister's father, our future king's father-in-law, the Kents in the country. There are peers a-go-go – Sutherland, Strathmore, Shaftesbury, Crawford, Milford and Gage, Glenconner, Erne and Cavendish. There are grandees from overseas: Heinz, Getty, Sackler and Said. Mick Jagger, Roger Waters, Lucian Freud, Antony Hobson the polyglot bibliophile, George Melly the surrealist jazzman and Geoffrey Bennison have all been clients. There is also the staple slew of merchants and bankers: Smiths, Barings, Hambros, Keswicks, Flemings and Sainsburys. Scattered throughout the kingdom are old and charming houses, most of them still lived in and loved by Nicky's clients; teased, tweaked and knocked into welcoming, comfortable, happy, family life.

He handles his clients, his colleagues and the builders and craftsmen who work with him with equal courtesy and clarity. Graham Porcher, from St Giles Joinery, remembers his patience, his sharp eye, his careful attention to every aspect of the job. "He's a real gentleman. He'd spend hours in the workshop, going over every detail. Not many architects do that." One cannot speak of Nicky's career without lauding the crucial role of his wife Susanna who, in the early years of their marriage, encouraged him to leave the drudgery of the big practice of which he was a part and emboldened her diffident man to set out on his own. Strong, merry, wise and kind, she has always been, and continues to be, the perfect counterpoint to his creative life.

16th March 2015

INTRODUCTION
Rosie Johnston

Nicholas John Johnston was born in Southsea in 1929, to Archibald and Pamela Johnston. His father was a naval captain stationed in Portsmouth.

NJJ was eight when his only brother Jeremy left for Dartmouth Naval College. That spring, NJJ developed an abscess on his hip with high temperatures that puzzled the local doctor. By summer, his condition had worsened and he was diagnosed with tuberculosis of the hip. Treatment consisted of draining the abscess each week and staying in bed, which he did for two and a half years.

The TB affected the bone and ate away the hip joint. Instead of a modern-day replacement, the bone was fused for strength without a cup-and-ball joint. NJJ's leg did not grow fully and he was left with a pronounced limp.

While bed-bound, NJJ studied the walls and ceilings of the hospital wards and sanatoriums. He became fascinated with how buildings worked; what went on behind the paint and plaster. He began to sketch, developing a sense of perspective and the ability to draw a straight line freehand. A visitor brought him a copy of Ralph Dutton's *The English Country House*

and so began a passion for historical architecture and old houses. By the time he was twelve, he knew he wanted to be an architect.

He went to Eton where he was taught drawing by Wilfred Blunt, and then to Cambridge to study architecture.

NJJ – "Cambridge taught me nothing practical. I never went on site, I never met a builder or a contractor. I had no idea of the nuts and bolts. Nowadays students probably deal with bricks and mortar at some point. I would have been totally bewildered. What I did learn was how many Doric pillars there were on the Parthenon."

NJJ left Cambridge to work for Guy Morgan in London. It was the early 1950s and architectural genres such as 'moderne' and 'international style', so popular 30 years before, were being rapidly replaced by Corbusian tower blocks.

NJJ – "It was the contemporary answer to social housing. In order to comply with the stringent rules about density on a site, you had to go up. Originally, there was a commitment to communal gardens at ground level – it took time to realise that those promised green spaces were just concreted over. We were all enthralled by Corbusier at the time, although I don't think anyone's done so much harm, architecturally."

Advocates of the New Brutalism such as Sir Denys Lasdun and Alison and Peter Smithson made an impression, as did the clean lines and decisive detailing of Soane's neoclassicism. Edwin Lutyens' imaginative adaptations of traditional British architectural styles were also influential, as was Edward Blore, with his precise understanding of Gothic and Norman revival design.

In 1961, encouraged by his wife Susanna, NJJ set up his own practice in the basement of their London house. It was around this time that he met the antique dealer and collector Christopher Gibbs with whom he has had a lifelong friendship and working association.

His first commissions were a kitchen for the pioneering cookery writer Arabella Boxer and a modern top storey for Simon Sainsbury's 18th-century London house. Both jobs featured in *The Sunday Times*.

In 1968, NJJ designed a series of kitchens and bedrooms for *The Observer* exhibitions. "The kitchens had sofas and hat stands. People thought it was barmy. Why would anyone want to sit surrounded by all that cooking?" The bedrooms had bunk beds, hammocks and under-bed drawers. By the end of the 1960s, domestic life in the UK

had changed dramatically. Live-in servants, back-room kitchens and children eating in the nursery were part of a bygone era as kitchens became the centre of the house. This paradigm was central to NJJ's practice, which grew rapidly at a time when Computer Assisted Drawing (CAD), office printers and photocopiers were unheard of.

NJJ – "The drawings were picked up in the morning, printed, then brought back in the afternoon with a terrific smell of chemicals. No firm our size had their own printers. We were haunted by deadlines and the London traffic."

Trevor Rich was the mainstay of the London office administration. In the early 1970s, NJJ met Peter Cave, who had a practice with his wife, Bryony. Peter took over the site work for Llanstephan in Pembrokeshire, and over the years became the linchpin for NJJ's architectural work.

Peter Cave – "NJJ had the clients, and he came up with the initial design concepts. I was able to support him with the resources and means with which to turn those concepts into reality.

"There was a critical element of interpretation in understanding NJJ's design ideas and turning them into something practical that could be built. I did that for him and so did others, notably Bob Gardner.

"NJJ is the master of design concept and his eye for fine detail is second to none. He sees clearly what's needed to make a design work, to make it right. In this respect, he's on a significantly higher level than all others working around him. His enthusiasm for chasing a design concept around knows no bounds. Ideas just keep coming. Far from being fazed when a client asks for late changes, he's always up for a challenge. I can't remember there being any sort of disagreement between us whatsoever."

Peter Cave and NJJ have worked together for 44 years. The final incarnation of their partnership, Johnston Cave Associates (JCA), is still a thriving practice thanks to Bryony Cave, Annie Bessy, Mike Clark, the late Bob Gardner, Rory Duncan, Chris Lawler, Nigel Hammett, Tony Sanger, Adrian Dadswell, Heather Berridge, Moira Claydon and others over the years. The firm is based at Henwood Studios, a collection of farm buildings outside Oxford, bought and converted by JCA in 1990.

NJJ – "Peter and the team made everything work beautifully so I could sit about sketching. It was Peter who knew we had to modernise. We were just starting Glympton in 1992. The job came to us via Philip Jebb who worked from his attic office at Bucklebury. He hadn't got the trace of a mechanisation and knew he never would, so he asked us to take over. CAD was jumped on by the office. It impacted everything although I've never used it. The drawings look dead – you have to go over them by hand to bring them to life."

Lyall Mews. First Floor

Now, NJJ is teaching one of the younger architects at JCA to draw as university courses only use CAD.

For 50 years, NJJ has sketched, schemed, converted, turned houses back-to-front, built from scratch and conjured planning permission from seemingly thin air.

While this book documents many houses still upright and happily lived in, some of NJJ's work has disappeared. Lyall Mews, the daringly modern house built for Henry and Margaret Vyner in the early 1970s, was pulled down in the 1980s leaving no record of its existence except the sketches shown below.

In today's world of the 'starchitect', stories of overspend and overstatement are rife. NJJ has never sought to make his mark. For him, architecture has not been a reflection of ego or grand design but a means of providing comfortable and practical shelter; of understanding and meeting the needs of his clients.

Adam Richards says, "In the trade, the collective noun for architects is jokingly known as a 'jealousy' of architects. Nicholas doesn't fit that mould at all. I first set up my practice in the spare room of a council flat and he encouraged me enormously. It meant so much to have advice and interest from someone as established as him."

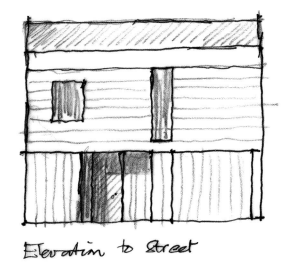

Elevation to Street

"Llanstephan has divided opinion since it was built."

LLANSTEPHAN HOUSE 1973

Hugo Philipps

SOUTH ELEVATION

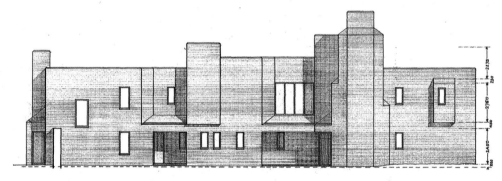

NORTH ELEVATION

The first Lord Milford gave Llanstephan to his grandson, Hugo Philipps, having disinherited Hugo's father for being a communist. The house had been built as a fishing lodge in the early 19th century but was greatly enlarged in 1920, much of the new fabric being reinforced concrete.

NJJ – "It was a white elephant, really. Much too big and pitch dark. Hugo didn't know what to do with it. He'd always wanted to build his own house, so eventually he decided to knock it down and start again." Hugo asked his old friend NJJ to work on schemes. NJJ – "The trouble with pulling down an existing house and putting up a new one in an established landscape – in this case against a hill surrounded by mature trees – is that the replacement is almost certainly on a smaller scale. I wanted the house to stand up to its surroundings

with the feeling of a border castle. The schemes were perfectly fanciful and idiotic to begin with, but we got it to two storeys and a tower."

When the time came, the demolition ball made no impression on Llanstephan's concrete walls; the wrecking team had to blow it up with dynamite. The first contractors went bust. The bricks were the wrong size.

NJJ – "Hugo was convinced it was old Lord Milford reaching out from the grave. But once we solved the brick problem and got going, it went pretty smoothly. We came in on budget – it was £110,000."

Llanstephan is arguably the closest NJJ's work has come to a contemporary architectural movement. Echoes of the New Brutalism, flourishing in the

early 1970s, are discernible in the dark brick walls and great glass windows on the south side. The arrow-slit windows and solid brick tower on the north side, however, look to the ancient Welsh castles of Gilbert St Clair and James St George. The entrance, to the left of the tower, is set back into the brick creating a shadowed recess.

NJJ – "I liked the idea of the entrance being forbidding – a bit of Welsh gloom – but once in, you're beckoned by a slot of light coming from the first floor. It's a taster of the view you're going to get, but you're so busy trying to see where you're going and where the staircase is, you don't dwell on it much. You go up the stairs, getting lighter and lighter, until you're on the landing looking over a spectacular turn in the Wye."

On the first floor, a bank of windows on the south side gives panoramic views of the valley and brooding Welsh hills beyond.

NJJ – "I'm not a fan of windows on the whole. Given that you have to have some, those work rather well. Hugo had a very bad back – his brief was to live on one floor as much as possible. We put his bedroom, the drawing room, dining room and kitchen on the first floor so he could enjoy the views. It did suit him. We used the service lift from the old house for groceries and wood coming up from the back door."

The children's rooms, playroom and spare rooms are on the ground floor. The tower holds another spare room.

Above: Llanstephan from across the field.

First Floor Landing + Terrace

*Right: The south side
showing the garden wall and
steps from the old house.*

Lower Hall. Looking to Bottom of
Stairs

*Right: The hall with a
shaft of light from the
first-floor window.*

Above: The north-facing entrance with the tower and arrow-slit windows.

Looking to Front Door from The Bank on North Side

Looking into Courtyard from Front Drive

Llanstephan is now lived in – and greatly admired and loved – by Hugo's son Guy Milford, his wife Alice and their two children.

NJJ – "My primary concern is always the idea of shelter; what the client's needs are. Llanstephan is straight-edged, very specifically built for Hugo. I'm amazed that two more generations are living there and enjoying it."

Hugo's grandson, Archie, describes the kitchen as "swag", but Llanstephan has divided opinion since it was built.

Alice Milford – "Often, when people come and visit us for the first time, we watch their cars drive past, stop and turn round. They've obviously looked at Llanstephan, decided we couldn't possibly live there and driven on. I really understood the house for the first time when I saw Caerphilly Castle in the mist."

NJJ – "I was at a dinner party; my neighbour asked me what I did. I told her I was an architect. 'It's so odd,' she replied, 'I live between two houses in Wales. One looks like a Georgian doll's house, the other like a chemical weapons factory, and they're both by the same architect.' 'Yes,' I replied. 'It was me.'"

Guy Milford – "I don't think we've had chemical weapons factory before. Municipal offices used to come up quite a lot, and a prison. But after 40 years, people are coming to respect the house for what it is."

Left: The corner window in the kitchen.

Above left: The kitchen.

*Above right: The
dining room.*

*Left: The drawing room
from the east.*

"The foundations were so insecure – everything was sliding about."

SHAW FARM

1979

Edward and Camilla Cazalet

Right: The drawing room.

Opposite page: The pavilion.

Shaw Farm's sensational position looks south over fields and woods to the Sussex Downs. The house was built on porous clay. When the Cazalets bought it in 1978, the foundations were in a parlous state.

NJJ – "Everything was sliding about. The floors were heaving."

Edward Cazalet – "Thanks to NJJ's perception of the extreme depth the builders had to go to secure the foundations, it's still upright. There isn't a crack anywhere."

NJJ – "Shaw Farm had all the potential to be a wonderful family house, but it was dark and low-ceilinged. We wanted to brighten things up.

We also removed some bay windows which gave a very busy feel."

NJJ enlarged the drawing room over a garden terrace and opened up a long passage from the drawing room to the staircase at the other end of the house. He moved the old front door from an awkward side-on position to the centre of the north side and topped it with a porch.

In 2000, NJJ designed a low-Gothic, weatherboard pavilion to house the kitchen for a flat joining the main house.

"He had so many wives, he had to sell his wyverns."

THE SWIMMING POOL IN MIDAIR

Late 1970s/early 1980s

Robert Heber Percy

Right: The castellated changing room.

Far right: The floor covered in old pennies.

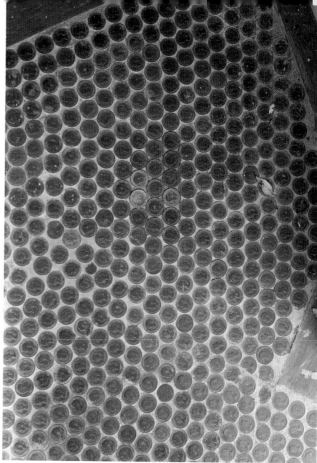

The following text is quoted from *The Mad Boy, Lord Berners, My Grandmother and Me** by Sofka Zinovieff.

"Other neighbours who frequently appeared were Susanna and Nicholas Johnston. Nicky had been the architect for what was probably Robert's greatest addition to the gardens – the 'stairs to nowhere' by the orangery, and the pool at the top of them. The great flight of stone steps surrounded by yew hedges was the first idea, built up a bank opposite the orangery and ending midair. This surreal tease was such a success that Robert decided to go one further and build a swimming pool up there. Nicky devised a way of incorporating a tank, and – after being rung in the middle of the night by Robert shouting, 'I want to go High Gothic' – then designed a castellated pepper-pot changing room with a floor of old pennies. Robert located a pair of very expensive 17th-century stone wyverns (winged, serpent-like dragons), that he bought with money won through gambling, and they were incorporated into the structure. The result was a triumph – Robert's own folly, created 40 years after Gerald (Berners) made his tower."

NJJ – "Robert bought the wyverns from Lord Kimberley. He had so many wives, he had to sell his wyverns. The building work was very slow – it could only be done when labour could be spared from the farm or when Jack Fox (the gamekeeper, builder and stonemason at Faringdon House) was free. It took years."

*Published by Jonathan Cape

"It was the ultimate
bachelor pad."

First Floor. Sitting room
Looking up steps to Dining Room

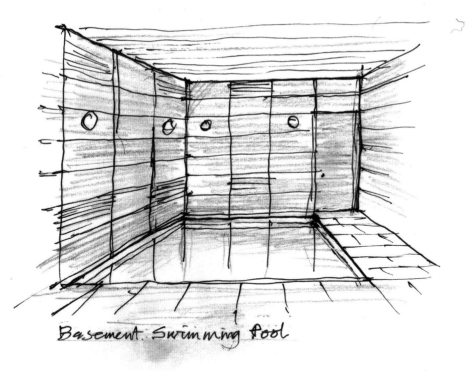

Basement: Swimming Pool

Ground Floor: Entrance Passage

DONNE PLACE

1982

Clive Sinclair

Photographs not by Christopher Sykes

Victoria Weymouth introduced NJJ to Clive Sinclair who had bought a disused warehouse in Donne Place. He wanted the conversion to include a garage, staff accommodation and a swimming pool and sauna in a building that was 16 feet wide. The warehouse was empty and had no garden or drive. The co-ordination and parking of heavy machinery was a thorny issue for the 15 months it took to complete. Planning permission was obtained on the proviso that the exterior remained looking like a warehouse and only showed three levels.

NJJ – "Clive Sinclair was very enthusiastic about our plans – he loved the tabula rasa aspect of it all – but there were endless difficulties fitting everything in. The big anxiety was digging so deep for the basement pool. We were only 30 feet from the Circle line."

Windows were a technical problem. It was illegal to have opening windows in boundary walls – they have to be frosted or opaque, fireproofed and sealed shut. NJJ created a narrow outside area at the back for windows to open out on.

The rooms and levels were centred around a stairwell with an adjacent lift shaft. The swimming pool, sauna and pool machinery room were in the basement. The raised ground floor housed the garage and the staff bedroom and bathroom were to the rear. The main reception room was on the first floor with a split level leading to the dining room beyond. NJJ designed a wooden bar-chest with deep drawers for bottles and glasses for the mezzanine because "there was nowhere else to put it" and a table and chest for the dining room. The kitchen was finished in black and white chrome. Clive Sinclair's bedroom had a

built-in hexagonal bathtub and a hexagonal skylight looking up to one of the two roof terraces divided by a sun room. Victoria Weymouth was responsible for the interior design of the bedroom, and consulted on the aesthetic treatment of the swimming pool.

NJJ – "We had a lovely time with the furniture design and detailing. We made the skirting boards flush with the polished plaster walls, which is a headache to do – it's much easier to add the skirting on top – but the effect creates beautiful shadows. It was the ultimate bachelor pad, really."

Top row, left to right: The kitchen. The dining room with furniture designed by NJJ, showing the corner window brought inwards so it could be opened. The garden room showing the roof terrace to the west.

Bottom row, left to right: The drawing room from the south. The drawing room from the north. The basement swimming pool.

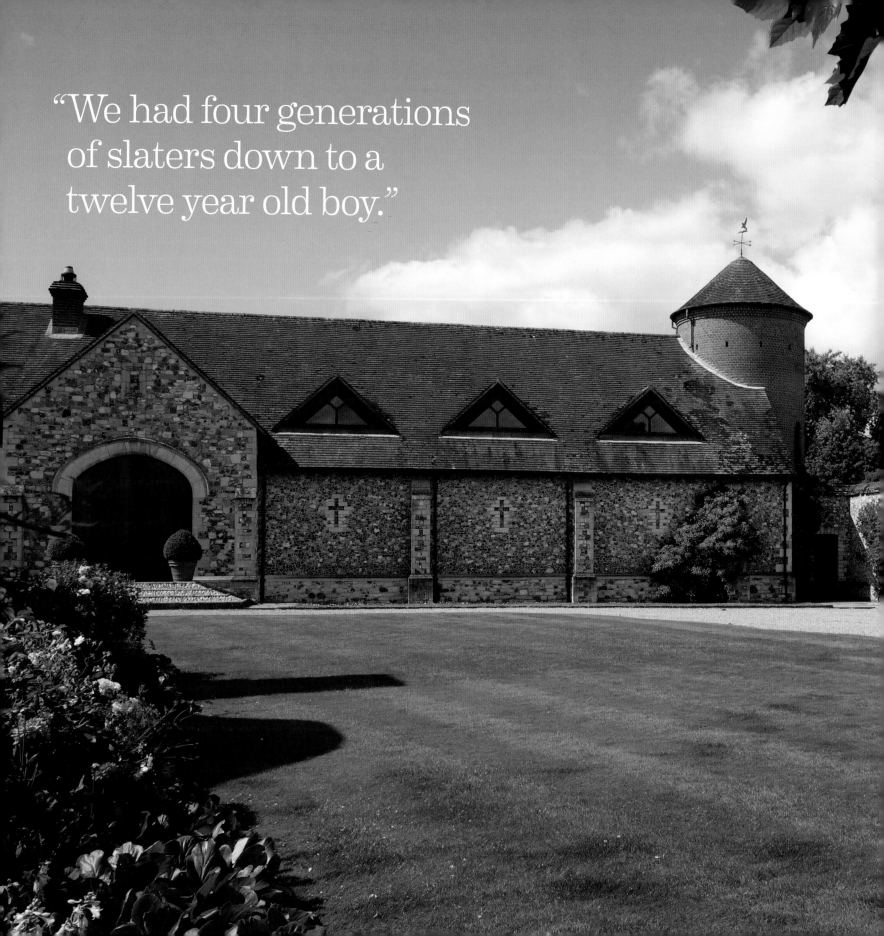

"We had four generations
of slaters down to a
twelve year old boy."

ROOKSNEST

1982

Parts of Rooksnest date back to 1560 but the house accrued major additions in the 1930s. When the owners bought it in 1982, they embarked on a major renovation programme. Victoria Weymouth introduced them to NJJ, although David Mlinaric did Rooksnest's interior design.

The restoration of the main house took four years and included putting a metal frame through two storeys to secure the structure. The four wings around a central courtyard did not complete a circuit through the house, so a cloister corridor was added to the east side to provide access from north to south. A breakfast room was added on to the north

side, and the western end of the Long Room was shortened to accommodate service cupboards.

The panelling was restored in several rooms but most notably in the dining room and the study. All the roof slates were redone. "We had four generations of slaters down to a twelve year old boy. I'm not sure why he wasn't at school," recalls the owner. "They were here for a year. Every slate was a different size, grading from small at the top downwards."

Over the following three years, JCA renovated various buildings on the estate including Willis Farm. The kitchen had a range with flatirons and

a well in the floor where the owners collected their water. JCA also designed and built a round-towered swimming pool adjoining the main house.

The owner – "NJJ was always responsive to our ideas and thoughts, always willing to give reasons why it should be one way or another. He never put his foot down and stamped – well, maybe once or twice if he was sure he was right, and he always was. The relationship between a client and architect is very personal; he was always so discreet, helpful and supportive."

Below: The main lobby before and after renovation.

Opposite page: Three arches with the main staircase in the middle. JCA created the wooden screen doors for the two outside arches.

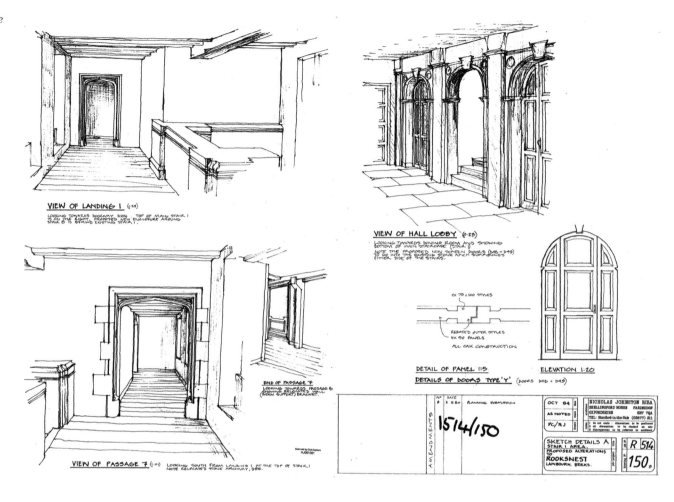

VIEW OF LANDING 1 (1·20)
LOOKING TOWARDS DOORWAY D104. TOP OF MAIN STAIR 1 IS ON THE RIGHT. PROPOSED NEW ENCLOSURE AROUND STAIR 8 IS BEHIND EXISTING STAIR 1.

VIEW OF HALL LOBBY (6·23)
LOOKING TOWARDS DINING ROOM AND SHOWING BOTTOM OF MAIN STAIRCASE (STAIR 1). NOTE THE PROPOSED NEW WOODEN DOORS (D48 + D49) TO GO INTO THE EXISTING STONE ARCH SURROUNDS EITHER SIDE OF THE STAIRS.

END OF PASSAGE 7
SHOWING RELOCATED WALL (ROOM SUPPORT) BRACKET.

VIEW OF PASSAGE 7 (1·01) LOOKING SOUTH FROM LANDING 1 AT THE TOP OF STAIR 1 NOTE RELOCATED STONE ARCHWAY, D56.

EX 75 × 100 STYLES

REBATED OUTER STYLES
EX 50 PANELS
ALL OAK CONSTRUCTION

DETAIL OF PANEL 1:5   ELEVATION 1:20
DETAILS OF DOORS TYPE 'Y' (DOORS D48 + D49)

1514/150

OCT 84   NICHOLAS JOHNSTON RIBA
AS NOTED   SHELLINGFORD HOUSE   FARINGDON
          OXFORDSHIRE   SN7 7QA
PC/NJ   TEL: Stanford-in-the-Vale (03677) 211

SKETCH DETAILS A   R 514
STAIR 1 AREA.
PROPOSED ALTERATIONS
TO
ROOKSNEST   150.B
LAMBOURN, BERKS.

"The job that
changed everything."

WORMSLEY

1984

Paul Getty

*Right: February 1985.
The entrance to the library
is neoclassical but has no
portico. The join from the
library to the house is drawn
as an extension of the house,
not the library.*

*To the right are schemes for
a cut through the woods to
create a view from the library
are on the right.*

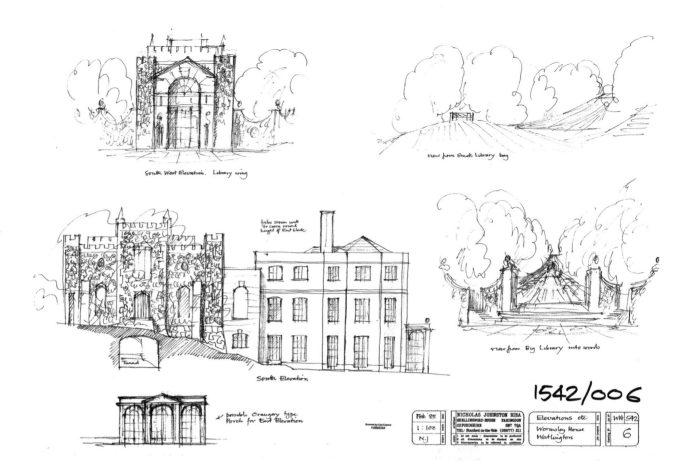

South West Elevation. Library wing

view from Small Library bay

South Elevation

view from Big Library into woods

possible Orangery type Porch for East Elevation

1542/006

In 1982, Paul Getty bought the Wormsley estate near Stokenchurch in the Chilterns. The house was so dilapidated that Nancy Lancaster, a friend of Wormsley's previous owner John Fane, could see what was going on downstairs through the floor in the upstairs lavatory.

Central to Getty's vision was his need to build a library worthy of his extraordinary and ever expanding collection of rare books and manuscripts. Christopher Gibbs, Getty's great friend and advisor, recommended NJJ.

Peter Cave – "NJJ and I went to Wormsley in 1982. It was then we realised the enormity of the job, it was a monstrously big undertaking for a small firm. We knew everything would have to change if we were going to do it."

Peter moved from Wales to Oxford, bringing four associates with him. He and NJJ took offices at Marsh Baldon, recruited another five workers and formed Johnston Cave Associates. "Everything was a bit haphazard until Peter took over the organisation," recalls NJJ. "He had the most wonderful grasp of how to make things work. It was a huge leap; we had no experience of doing anything as big as this."

Wormsley is an arcadian paradise in a valley hidden by towering beech trees. Oaks cover the clay cap; great cedars and old yews stand by the house. On a site visit with Christopher Gibbs, NJJ realised that the library "should look as if it were there before everything else, not a postmodern add-on that would clamour for attention." Their vision of the library as towered and turreted took hold. The idea was supported and encouraged by Richard Smith, the architectural

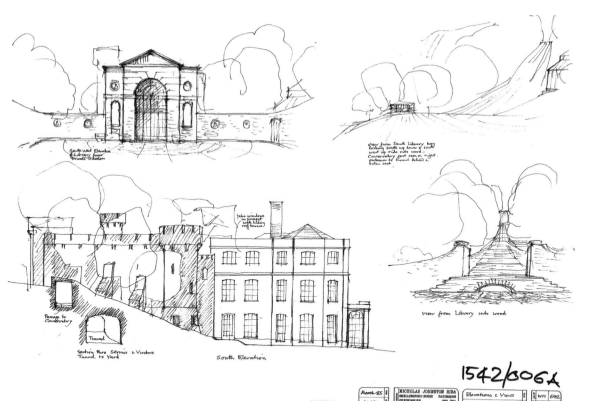

Left: March 1985.
The hinge from the library to
the house has been reduced
and incorporated into the
library fabric, rather than
the house. The visitors'
tunnel and passage to the
conservatory are shown
under the library.

South West Elevation of Library from Tunnel Garden

view from Small Library looking south up tower & south-west up side into wood. Conservatory part seen on right. entrance to tunnel behind below seat.

view from Library into wood

Passage to Conservatory

Tunnel

Section thro' Service & Visitors Tunnel to Yard

South Elevation

false windows in parapet with hidden roof terrace

1542/006A

March 85 — NICHOLAS JOHNSTON RIBA — SHELLINGFORD HOUSE — FARINGDON — OXFORDSHIRE — SN7 7QA — TEL: Stanford-in-the-Vale (03677) 211 — Elevations & Views — Wormsley House — Watlington — WM 542 — 6A

Courtyard. New Door on East side. North Passage & South Bathrooms removed.

Library Tower & Fourth Elevation seen from South East

new from South

Library looking towards S.W. Window

Orangery Porch on East Elevation - (Part Elevation)
Scale 1:100

yes - show progression of library.

1542/008

advisor to Wycombe District Council. He was critical to the project's success with the local authority, as the original listed building was increased in volume by 250 per cent – a rare achievement.

NJJ – "The handling of the library was influenced by my experience of working on Crom Castle in County Fermanagh, designed by Edward Blore. We used Blore as a basis for the doors, architraves, skirting, panelling and other joinery details of the library."

NJJ's sketches for the library façade, interior and hinge to the main house went through various schemes; the hinge became the conservatory and then the tower. A rotunda with four doors resolved the angle where the library joins the house.

The final scheme was a cathedral-style vault with a rectangular ceiling. European and English oak were used for the beams and had to be cut in one tranche to avoid visible joins.

Christopher Gibbs and NJJ decided on flint quarried from the Chilterns for the exterior cladding. Peter Cave oversaw the flint work.

PC – "It was an immense task, the biggest UK flint project since Goodwood House in the 18th century. We covered 2,000 square metres."

Several factors contributed to the flint being laid in bands and sections. "We couldn't get enough matching flint from any one source. It came from all over the place, even beaches on the south coast.

Looking from library out
through portico to sloping bank

Courtyard with
single storey Front Hall
& "cleaned up" main wall

Looking back to south west corner
of house with library let into
rising ground to west

Looking down on
house & library - to left

1542/014

We ended up with a very mixed bag of sizes, colours and shapes. They had to be sorted out, then designed into the external elevational treatment of bands and plinths and quoins, then the pinnacles and special dressings."

Eddie Finken and his son Ron (EdRon) spent six months in an Old Testament-style tent at the bottom of the drive, knapping, grading and storing the flint before a piece was laid.

PC – "We (JCA) led and co-ordinated the flint but there was huge input from Eddie Finken and his team, the structural engineers (David Osborne), the quantity surveyors (Yves Allier), and our builders, Holloway White Allom Ltd."

Chester Jones designed the library's interior. His team carried out painstaking research and, with Jones' draftsman Vincent Matthews, brought interpretations of Blore's work to life with meticulous Gothic detail.

The 19th-century fireplace was designed by Sir Charles Barry for Bowood House. Above it, Christopher Hobbs' wind vane frames a map of the estate. The ceiling was decorated with the astrological conjunction from the day of Paul Getty's birth. Christopher Gibbs' splendid furnishings include a table from William Beckford's Fonthill and another designed by Philip Webb. Chester Jones found the mighty stag's head, designed the carpet inspired by a marble pavement and sourced other furnishings and pieces.

Above: The portico is added for the library entrance. The hinge between the house and library is elongated further. The library has a barrel-vaulted ceiling.

Above: The library ceiling.

Opposite page: The flint cladding on the library exterior.

Chester Jones – "NJJ is a gentleman with absolute understanding of the grammar of design, of classical English vernacular. He saw things as a joint effort. If I felt something wasn't working, he listened."

Behind its neo-Norman, flint-clad exterior, the Wormsley library is a state-of-the-art, rigorously regulated building.

PC – "The insurers and security consultants wanted arrangements that were incompatible with the design and at odds with the way Sir Paul wanted to use his library. The technical advisors were horrified by the idea of an open fireplace. A special shutter was designed to close it off instantly in the event of a fire alarm. It was only meant to be open when Sir Paul was having a log fire. On one occasion the shutter slammed down at the wrong time. After that, he ordered it to be fixed open permanently and the insurers and security people had to live with it."

Air-sampling systems were used to detect smoke and heat in the event of fire. The fire-fighting medium was halon gas, programmed to be released into the library within seconds of a fire being detected. Halon pushes oxygen out of the atmosphere, replacing it with a gas that doesn't support fire or flame, but it is deadly to humans. It was later replaced by a more manageable inert gas.

The books need constant, highly-regulated air movement drawn through the backs of the bookcases. These technical requirements affected every aspect of their construction, joinery and detailing. NJJ designed the library's external flying buttresses to house air-conditioning ducts.

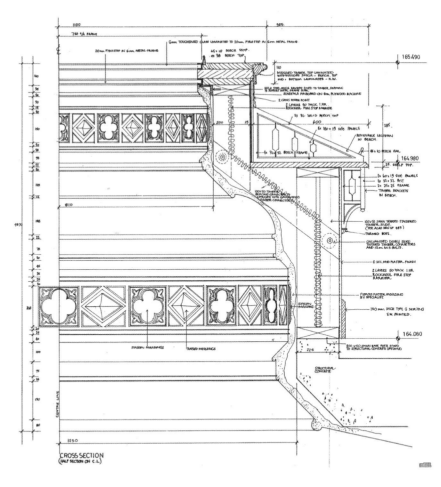

The temperature and humidity of the library interior and the bookstore below were kept to stringent limits via a vast plant room full of chillers and an air-handling plant. The hugely intricate control system was integrated into a building-management system complex for the house and library. The M&E services consultants were Cundall Johnston, led by Laurie Clark, with whom JCA worked closely.

Wet services (WCs and kitchens) were banned from the library building in case of water damage from leaking pipes.

Behind the main house was a rear courtyard that became the delivery and maintenance point for the library.

PC – "We went through a number of options for accessing this service courtyard. We decided on a rear drive in an open cutting through the chalk at the back. We did this, but Sir Paul and Christopher Gibbs didn't like the steep chalk sides to the cutting, so we made an architectural and landscape feature by bridging it over."

Julian and Isabel Bannerman created the rustic treatment of the tunnel, lining it with tufa rock for a dramatic, Piranesi effect. Tufa is also used for the bridge that JCA designed to carry the drive over the join between the two lakes devised by the Bannermans.

Above left: Detail of the rotunda ceiling.

Above right: Detail of the joinery plans for the library.

Opposite page: The recess and plinth by the library entrance.

The Cricket Pavilion

NJJ – "We had two stabs at it. The centre block is the original. The inside was a basic milling around and changing space, but the pitch became increasingly popular, so we enlarged it by adding a wing on either side."

The steps descending towards the pitch from the pavilion are paved with hearts of oak, inspired by the 18th-century riding school at Hovingham in Yorkshire.

The Wormsley estate is now run by Mark Getty. Garsington Opera has a permanent theatre there and the cricket ground, one of the most beautiful in the world, is used frequently for first-class and international matches. The library is run by Bryan Maggs, who helped Paul Getty compile his extraordinary collection of rare books and manuscripts. The rarest items, including Anne Boleyn's psalter and Caxton's printing of *The Canterbury Tales*, are regularly displayed for visitors on cricket-match days.

Left: Detail of the bat and wicket balustrade designed by NJJ for the cricket pavilion.

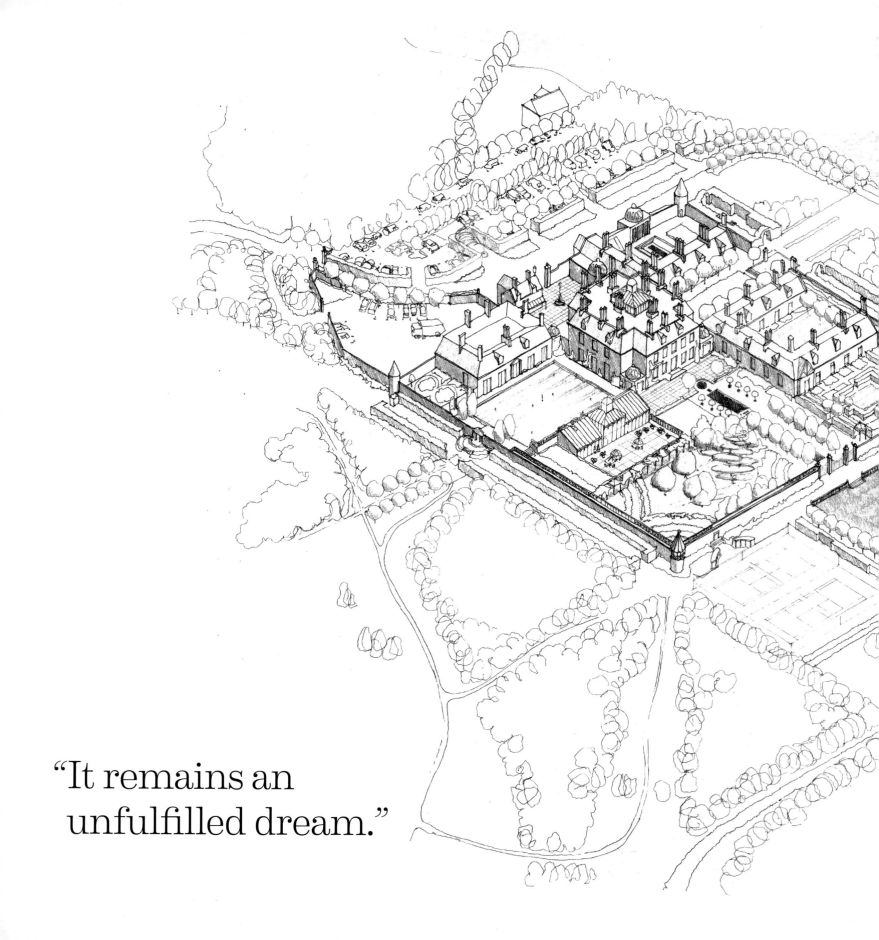

"It remains an
unfulfilled dream."

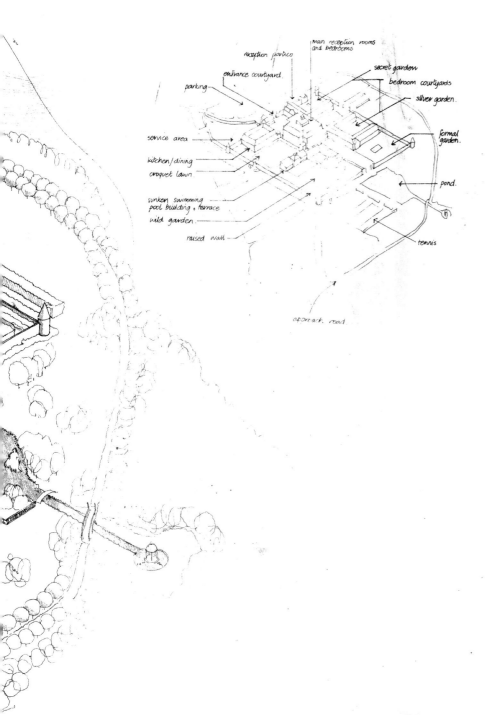

main reception rooms
and bedrooms

reception portico

entrance courtyard

secret garden

parking

bedroom courtyards

silver garden

service area

formal
garden

kitchen/dining

croquet lawn

pond.

sunken swimming
pool building + terrace

wild garden

tennis

raised walk

approach road

RUSHMORE HOTEL PROJECT 1987

RUSHMORE HOTEL

NICHOLAS JOHNSTON RIBA.   NOVEMBER 1987

Above left: The view of the entrance canopy is reminiscent of one of the existing wall arbours.

Above right: Looking towards the south front. The bedroom wing is on the right.

The Rushmore Hotel project was conceived by Simon Elliot and Jonathan Crawley as a luxurious weekend destination with all the connotations of a grand country house. Simon Elliot – "Michael Pitt Rivers, who owned the land we wanted to develop, was a very autocratic figure. He used a voice box because of throat cancer, which could make discussions difficult. As partners in the Rushmore project, we envisaged a new hotel in the old walled garden, an adjoining golf course, access to the stud stables and possible syndication of the shooting rights over 2,000 acres."

JCA were invited to submit schemes along with five other architectural firms.

NJJ – "We won, which was terribly exciting. The leisure side of Guinness was on board, everything was going ahead. We worked on the schemes and started the planning application, which wasn't easy as it was an Area of Outstanding Natural Beauty. We asked the planning committee to come to the site and see how suitable it was for our kind of development. When the walk round was over, the chairman of the committee – a rather formidable lady – had a car boot full of eggs she wanted to sell. I bought trays and trays of eggs I didn't want because I thought it would help our case."

SE – "JCA were awarded the contract not only for their designs but because they used the space in the best possible way, with a sympathetic approach coming through the woods. It was commercial in its layout as well as being functional from an operator's standpoint. A further factor was JCA's considered approach to the planners. Our judgement on this was rewarded as we were granted outline planning permission."

The main body of the hotel was to be three storeys high with an 18th-century feel, redolent of Kingston Lacy or Ashdown House. The facilities were to include a swimming pool in a huge glass orangery, underground tennis courts, a croquet lawn, a reflecting pool and a conference centre all within the vast walled garden.

By the end of the 1980s, however, the world economy was jittery. The planning permission was on the verge of coming through when the investors pulled out and the project was shelved.

SE – "It could have been the Gleneagles of the south of England. The golf course went ahead but sadly the hotel wasn't, and probably never will be, built. It remains an unfulfilled dream."

Top left: The first view of the buildings from the approach road along a vista angled on the southwest corner pavillion.

Top right: A second view of the building through the main south screen from the bridge

over the new pond outside the walls.

Bottom left: Looking south to the bridge of the approach road.

Bottom right: Inside the cobbled forecourt.

"Our conservation officer was notoriously difficult. She sat behind a bulletproof screen."

BISHOPS BARN 1987

Piers and Susy Brooke

Above: Bishops Barn from the west. The garden and parterre were laid out by Michael Balston.

In 1987, Bishops Barn consisted of an early 18th-century cottage with a 20th-century 'hump' in a sensational position in the remote countryside beyond Hungerford. The brief was to knock down the addition and build a house with a drawing room, study, large kitchen, six bedrooms, three bathrooms and a gents.

Planning permission proved tricky. The council was convinced that Bishops Barn lay on a virgin site because of a piece of flint wall standing unattached in a field that is now the garden – there was speculation that it was part of an ancient building. Local workmen insisted that there was an underground tunnel leading to a church that had existed at the time of the first bishop.

NJJ suggested that flint walls have a signature and this might give a clue as to who had built it and when. It turned out to be a man called Norman, very much alive, whose mother had looked out over his brother's scrapheap and said, "Norman, build me a wall!"

Susy Brooke – "There's a huge car scrapyard buried under the present tennis court. Each time a car rusts and falls apart the tennis court sinks, but the council had gone on about it being a virgin site."

NJJ – "We still had to get permission for increased capacity. Our conservation officer was notoriously difficult. She sat behind a bulletproof screen; you could only get through by logging in a password. As it happened, someone did get through and thumped her because they were having such a horrible time."

Left: The garden room's Gothic detail door and windows.

Below: The kitchen through to the garden room.

SB – "NJJ came up with a wonderful narrative to help me envisage the new house. 'Imagine it as a dower house,' he said. 'The duchess is being slotted into the deer-keeper's cottage by her son, who can't wait to get her out'. She would have said, 'I simply can't exist without proper ceilings, proper cornices and sash windows.'" Everything followed on from that; what the dowager duchess would have wanted."

The level of the lawn to the south of the old cottage was lowered to create the height the drawing room needed. The arched, Gothic windows give an early 19th-century feel and the east side of the hall shares the thick, outside wall of the old cottage. In 1992, NJJ added a garden room to the kitchen to increase the kitchen's area.

Top: A sketch scheme for the conversion of the drawing room into a large family kitchen/living room.

Above: The drawing room from the west. NJJ designed the fireplace. The carpet was designed by Piers Brooke and made in Afghanistan.

Right: Bishops Barn cupboards and bookshelves with Gothic detailing.

SB – "It makes the garden a part of the house. The light streams in, as it does everywhere in the house. NJJ is very aware of light; of what it will do to a room."

NJJ is currently converting another building – The Little Barn – into a dower cottage and working on a possible rethink of the drawing room and study in light of what a new generation might need. The putative scheme is to knock them into one large family room with a kitchen, dining room and sofas.

SB – "I put it to NJJ, worried about what he'd think of a plan to alter his work, but he said that houses have to change. It was such a wonderful response."

NJJ – "It's terribly flattering. I've never been asked to renovate a house that I've built."

SB – "We had such fun doing Bishops Barn. My strongest memories are of the many, many laughs."

Top: A sketch for the hall and staircase.

Above: The hall and staircase as they are now.

*Right: A sketch showing the
old cottage on the right, facing
south, with the new hall and
drawing room extension on
the left.*

*Below: Bishops Barn as it
is now.*

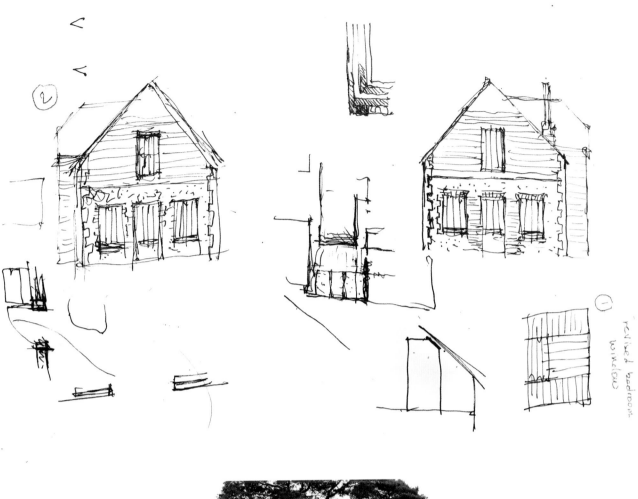

Left: A sketch showing plans for the conversion of The Little Barn.

Below: The Little Barn as it is now.

"He was affable but a big spender."

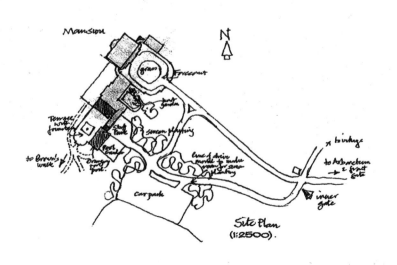

Site Plan
(1:2500).

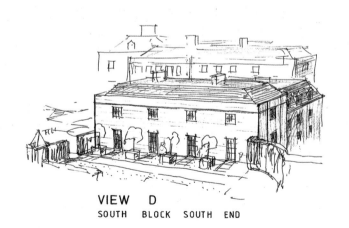

VIEW D
SOUTH BLOCK SOUTH END

NUNEHAM
PARK   1988

1638/0005

NICHOLAS JOHNSTON RIBA	
SHELLINGFORD HOUSE	FARINGDON
OXFORDSHIRE	SN7 7QA
TEL: Stanford-in-the-Vale	(036 77) 211

PROJECT: NUNEHAM HOUSE

SHEET TITLE: SKETCH SCHEME 'A'
VIEW FROM SOUTH WEST.

DO NOT SCALE : DIMENSIONS TO BE PREFERRED
ALL DIMENSIONS TO BE CHECKED ON SITE
DISCREPANCIES TO BE REFERRED TO ARCHITECT

JAN '89	DATE	AMENDMENT	JOB	0638
NJ	DRAWN		DWG. No.	5
N.T.S.	SCALE			

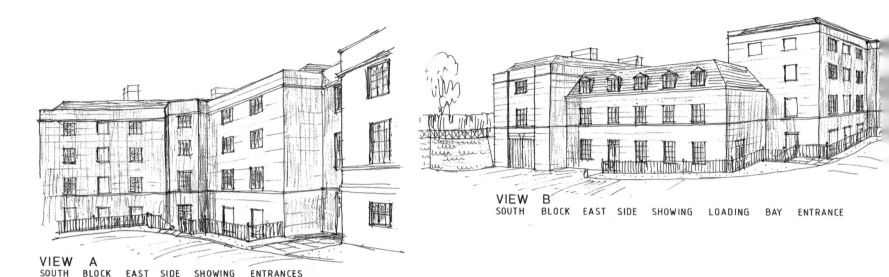

VIEW A
SOUTH BLOCK EAST SIDE SHOWING ENTRANCES

VIEW B
SOUTH BLOCK EAST SIDE SHOWING LOADING BAY ENTRANCE

Nuneham Park was built by the first Earl Harcourt in 1756. The architect, Stiff Leadbetter, designed a square Palladian house with two small wings beautifully sited above a turn in the river Thames at Stanton Harcourt, near Oxford.

It was conceived as a rustic idyll so fashionable for grand families at the time, although the earl had no intention of compromising on comfort or formality.

He removed the entire village of Nuneham Courtney to a location along the main Oxford road because it disrupted his view. Capability Brown laid out the original garden which, over the years, developed into a semi-romantic roam through a classical landscape with hidden statues and a magnificent arboretum.

The house was significantly altered by Henry Holland in the 1780s. In 1848, Dr William Buckland, the renowned theologian, genealogist and zoophagist* visited Nuneham. He was shown a shrivelled object in a silver box by the second Earl Harcourt. Before anyone could stop him, Buckland swallowed it whole, only to learn he'd eaten the mummified heart of Louis XIV, stolen by grave robbers during the French Revolution. Buckland reportedly said that a dash of marmoset gravy would have improved the flavour.

!n 1904, Nuneham went to Vernon Harcourt, a prominent liberal politician, after the death of his older brother and nephew. He had introduced death duties in 1894, jeeringly called 'the younger brother's revenge' as at the time he had nothing to inherit. The estate was in disarray, mainly because of the

VIEW C
TERRACES & DINING ROOM SOUTH FACADE

taxes owed on it, and Harcourt died there the same year he inherited. His son, Louis Harcourt (Loulou) was married to JP Morgan's niece, Mary Burns**. Her money hauled Nuneham out of debt and funded extensive renovations and additions. Loulou's predatory paedophilia undid him, however. His predilections had been noted for years, but in 1921 the mounting whispers surrounding his attempted assault on a young Edward James, the future millionaire patron of the surrealists, threatened disgrace. Loulou committed suicide by drinking a bottle of Bromidia.

The estate was sold to Oxford University in the 1950s.

NJJ – "In 1988, we were approached by the head of a hotel group*** to develop Nuneham Park as a hotel. He was affable but a big spender; if he could possibly go somewhere in a helicopter, he would. When he had a working lunch, it was at Le Manoir aux Quat'Saisons." JCA presented extensive schemes and everything was in place when The Big Spender restructured the company and bolted to the United States, indemnifying himself against huge financial commitments to the investors. His partners claimed the indemnity was obtained fraudulently, the project collapsed and protracted law suits rolled out on both sides of the Atlantic.

Nuneham is now a spiritual retreat centre with no public access to the house or gardens.

* One who eats his way through the animal kingdom.

** Mary Burns was cousin May to Sylvia Paget, NJJ's mother-in-law. She spent many days at Nuneham.

*** Name withheld.

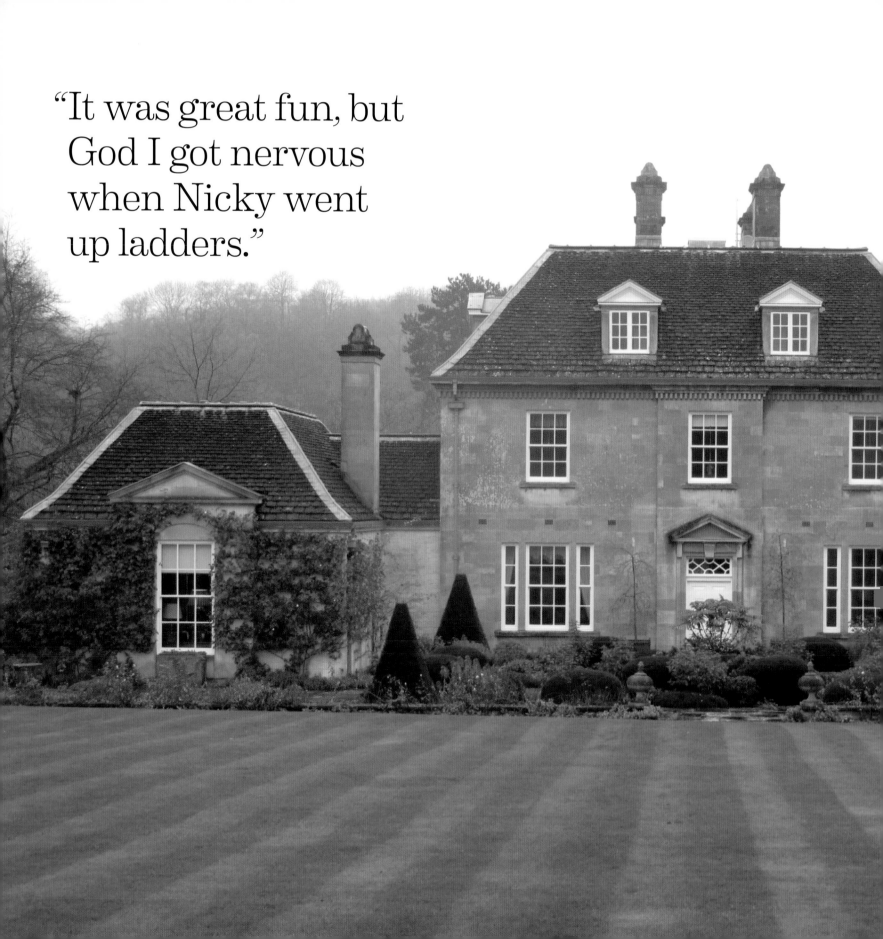

"It was great fun, but God I got nervous when Nicky went up ladders."

ROCKCLIFFE

1991

Simon and Emma Keswick

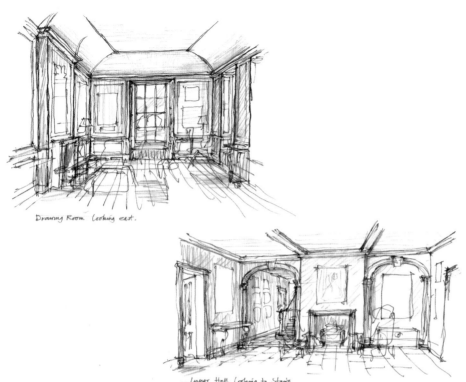

Drawing Room. Looking east.

Inner Hall Looking to Stairs

Looking from Front Door towards Inner Hall

Rockliffe was built in 1860, as a dower house for Eyford House.

NJJ – "The house was very four-square. We added two wings of a slightly different size, dictated by the fact that we couldn't go further than a certain point on the north side, and on the south we wanted a slightly bigger room. We turned the house round. The front door was where you'd expect it to be but you couldn't drive up to it, so invariably people went to the back door. We put in a little square outer hall and a Gothic passage."

Emma Keswick – "We lived in the house for a year before we started work, to get the seasons, the wind, the light. We added a drawing room and an orangery in one extension; the other extension gave us an outer hall, inner hall, boot room and library.

We live in one and the other is for when we have guests. They work really well; you can heat them independently. The building took a year to the day. It was great fun, but God I got nervous when Nicky went up ladders."

In 2001, NJJ and Bob Gardner designed and built the dovecote in a field on the north side of the house. It was the last job that Bob Gardner did; he died soon after of cancer. NJJ – "I met Bob when he was working as a draughtsman for the first stage of Rockliffe in the 1970s. Soon after that he set up on his own. I started off advising him on what to draw but he picked it up so fast, he knew exactly what to do. Bob had an extraordinary way of interpreting preliminary thoughts for a design. He was a lovely chap."

Far left: The drawing room.

Left: Topiary birds in the garden leading up to the dovecote.

Below: The orangery.

"The renovations took three years and over a hundred skilled craftsmen and builders."

DANEWAY

1993

Nick and Kai Spencer

In 1993, Nick and Kai Spencer fell in love with a small, Cotswold-stone manor house hidden away in a Gloucestershire valley. They bought Daneway thinking it needed six months of work – the house had no central heating or insulation and barely functioning plumbing and electrics. The renovations took three years and over a hundred skilled craftsmen and builders. The challenge was immense – five new bathrooms, a new underground extension for service areas to complement the small, medieval kitchen, the integration of the 1315 great hall with a late 14th-century parlour, a reversion of a late 19th-century staircase to its original medieval form and direction and a raft of other revisions, all while preserving the extraordinary ancient fabric of the house. One of the most daring changes, according to NJJ, was dropping the end of the dining room by five inches to correct an unworkable tilt in the floor.

Daneway's oldest structure dates back to 1315, when the great hall and solar were built for the Clifford family. Over the centuries there have been inevitable refinements and additions, the most significant being the imposing High Tower in 1674, possibly conceived as an eccentric bachelor pad for an unmarried son. The tower's remarkable plaster friezes were restored as part of the renovation work.

"One of NJJ's many strengths as an architect, particularly with a building the age of Daneway, is his extraordinary attention to detail," says Nick Spencer. "Nothing escapes his eye."

NJJ – "The gentleman plasterers used the proper lyme-plastering process, which is incredibly slow. Each layer has to dry before the next one is put on and it can't be too thick. There were often a number of well-

Above: The kitchen and flower room, before.

The kitchen had been an 18th-century wash-house. The ground surface level was at kitchen ceiling level to the north and east. The proposal was to burrow underground to extend the kitchen's utility area as an overground extension wasn't permitted by English Heritage.

Left: The view to the kitchen from the flower room as it is now.

Left: The great hall, before, showing the Oliver Hill window and the door into the High Tower.

Above: NJJ's proposal for a platform from the door to the High Tower to meet an old oak door, which was at a higher level than the (then) existing floor. It would increase floor area and remove a gully behind the proposed place for the sofa. The platform would have to be 'removable' to get past English Heritage.

educated young men sitting around eating sandwiches, discussing their next shooting weekend." Nick Spencer recalls that meetings with NJJ and the contractors during winter were sometimes moved to the garden, where it was warmer than inside the stone house.

Because of its Grade I listing, the restoration of Daneway involved numerous and convoluted dealings with English Heritage and Stroud District Council. NS – "They went to extraordinary lengths to make it seem as if nothing had changed. There were men up trees taking photographs to make sure you couldn't see the swimming pool from the house. NJJ guided us through with exceptional patience and knowledge." The swimming pool is hidden by a wall with four different turrets designed by NJJ. The original garden was laid out by Oliver Hill and Vita Sackville-West to mirror a series of small, medieval rooms. Mary Keen restored it, adding yew-tree walks and hidden sculptures.

Above left: The great hall, or drawing room, as it is now. The oak door opens on to Nick Spencer's study.

Left: The hall.

Above: The proposed layout of furniture to show how the platform would work.

Right: Looking back at the staircase from the upper chamber.

Far right: Looking back to the window and stairs coming up from the ground floor.

Bottom left: NJJ's designs for the bun-feet lavatory and sink.

Bottom right: As it is now.

Opposite page, top left: The stairs looking back from the upper chamber, before.

Opposite page, bottom left: Looking through to the upper chamber with NJJ's proposal to turn the staircase back to its original orientation. It had been altered in the 1960s.

Opposite page, far right: The staircase, after.

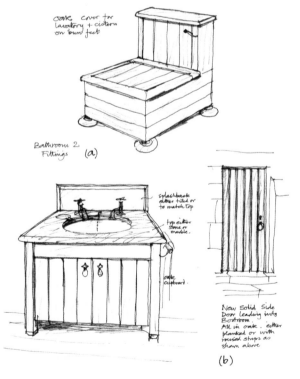

Oak cover for lavatory + cistern on bun feet

Bathroom 2 Fittings   (a)

Splashback either tiled or to match top

top either stone or marble.

oak cupboard

New Solid Side Door leading into Bedroom. All in oak. either planked or with raised steps as shown above

(b)

Top left: The upper chamber, before.

Top right: As it is now. The roof-void closets could not be permanent structures or inhibit the view of the ceiling.

Above: Sketches and before-renovation images of the bathroom. A sample taken from a beam in this bathroom dates Daneway to 1315. Planning application included the argument that the beams would be seen by people having a bath, not hidden away in a cupboard.

Above left: The view to the kitchen from the flower room.

Above: A bedroom conversion.

Left: The informal dining room. To the left is the foot of the altered staircase.

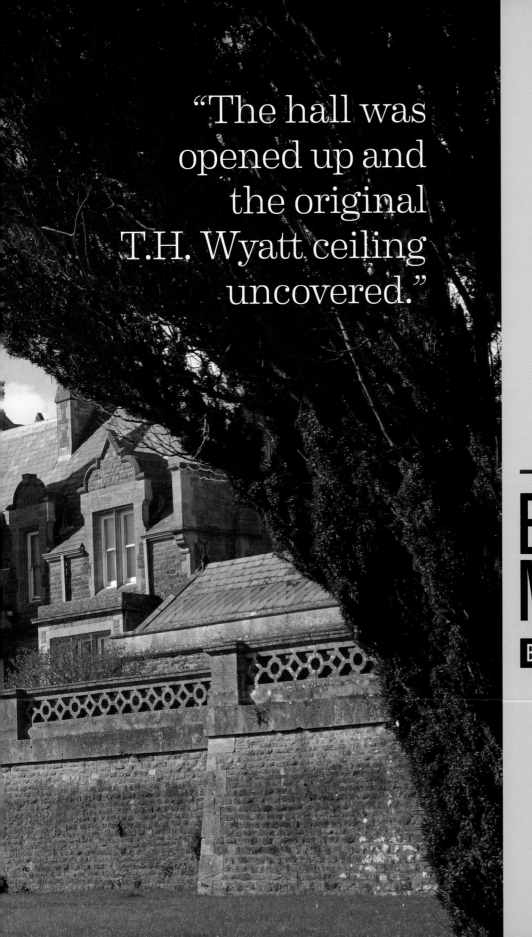

"The hall was opened up and the original T.H. Wyatt ceiling uncovered."

EDON
MANOR
1993

Brandon and Eileen Wang

Right: The new arch, pilasters and passage facing the hall.

Far right: The upstairs gallery.

Edon Manor was built as Kitemore House by Thomas Henry Wyatt in 1860, with later alterations in 1910 and 1920. When Eileen and Brandon Wang bought it in 1992, they knew the house needed a significant overhaul. Original Wyatt gables were missing, the roof had lost its proportions and an earlier owner had the magnificent chimneys lowered, as the noise of the wind in the stacks disturbed him.

NJJ – "There was a huge competition for the job of rebuilding Kitemore and redesigning the approach. The old drive went along and back the same way. Our scheme showed the drive looping round so you saw the house, lost sight of it and then pulled up slantingly to the front door.* We had a cut through the wood with a canal lake, all of which turned out to be champion feng shui. It won us the job, although I had no idea, of course."

Inside, the hall was opened up and the original T.H. Wyatt ceiling uncovered. A staircase to the right of the main door to the hall was removed. A new arch was created to the right of the entrance with pilasters on either side.

NJJ – "As it was, the approach to the long passage to the later addition was squashed into the corner of the hall so you couldn't put a piece of furniture there. We took some liberties, moving the approach into the middle so you didn't look down the passage all at once. You go through the arch, turn left and get another vista."

Tom Stuart-Smith designed the canal lake, Lucy Ward did the interiors. The reconstruction of Edon Manor took two years.

* The main façade is on the other side of the house, facing south.

Left: The hall.

Below: The north side, showing the canal lake from the drive which curves around the wood in both directions.

"I actually rather
dreaded it."

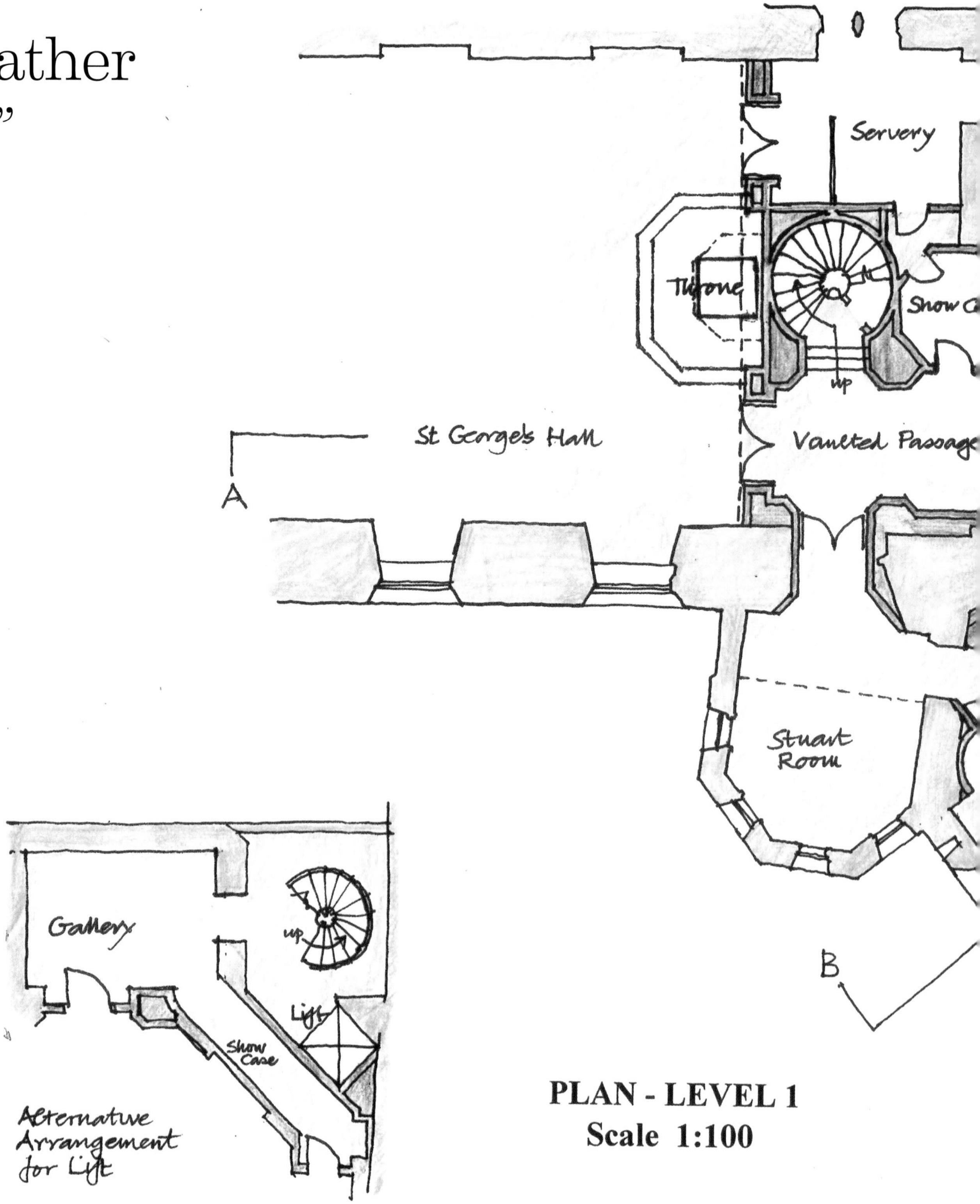

Servery

Throne

Show C

St George's Hall

A

Vaulted Passage

Stuart
Room

Gallery

up

Lift

Show
Case

B

Alternative
Arrangement
for Lift

PLAN - LEVEL 1
Scale 1:100

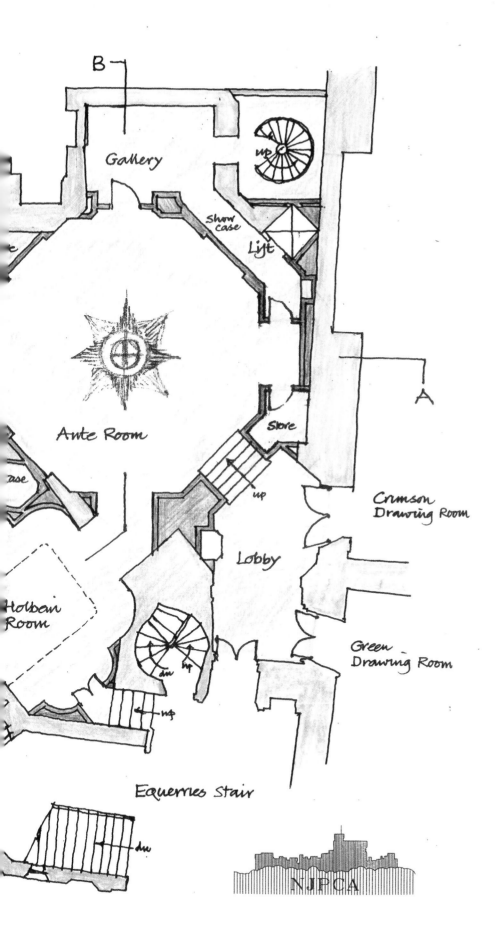

WINDSOR CASTLE FIRE RESTORATION SCHEME 1993

The Royal Palaces

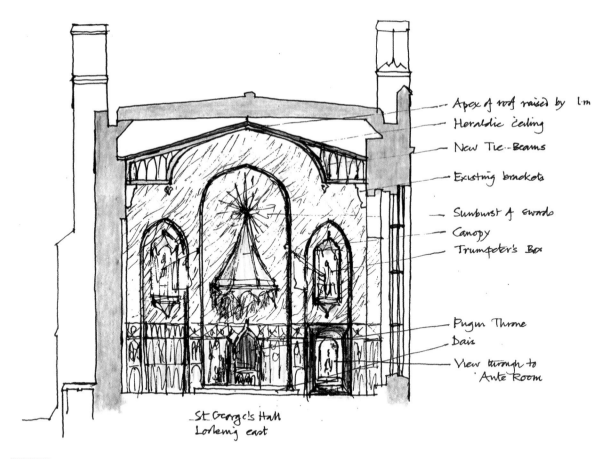

Apex of roof raised by 1·m
Heraldic ceiling
New Tie-Beams
Existing brackets
Sunburst & swords
Canopy
Trumpeter's Box
Pugin Throne
Dais
View through to Ante Room

St George's Hall
Looking east

JCA, along with three other small architectural firms, were invited to enter a limited competition organised by the Royal Palaces for the refurbishment and rebuilding of designated areas of Windsor Castle after the fire in 1992. JCA's scheme was presented at a meeting overseen by Donald Insall, who was in charge of the post-fire restoration work. Over half the damaged and destroyed rooms, including the State and Octagon dining rooms, were to be restored to their original state.

In the end, Sidell Gibson was awarded the contract for the reconstruction of St George's Hall, the Queen's Private Chapel and the Stuart and Holbein room.

NJJ – "I didn't think we would get it and I actually rather dreaded it. It would have been all-consuming and quite tricky."

Level 2. Gallery. Looking towards top of free-standing spiral stairs.

Looking west

Level 1. Ante Room. Looking towards St George's Hall

"He produced plans
for a house that he'd
shaped to our lives."

THE OLD RECTORY, EAST WOODHAY 1994

Peter and Tessa Baring

Photographs not by Christopher Sykes

Above left: The Little Coach House.

PB – *"He worked out that if you raised the building by two brick courses, you'd get an extra room in. It went from a two-bedroom cottage to three bedrooms.*

Above right: The Little Coach House.

Peter and Tessa Baring bought the Old Rectory, East Woodhay, in 1993. Built in 1828 using red brick in the Flemish bond style, the Grade II listed house has a glorious, elevated position overlooking its garden and surrounding fields. Peter Baring – "NJJ told us to live in the house for a year before we started work on it. That gave us time to decide what we wanted to do, with his advice. He produced plans for a house that he'd shaped to our lives."

A main requirement was a big, family kitchen. The old dining room and ground floor gents were knocked through, uniting three floor-to-ceiling Gothic Revival windows in one large room. An island that had kitchen surfaces on the cooking side was disguised as a desk with cupboards on the dining side, but was also a functioning sideboard. The window farthest east was turned into French doors, with steps leading down to the garden.

The walled garden had a section nearest the house that was not in keeping with the rest of it. Planners refused permission to rebuild in flint, saying that it was the original wall and should be kept the way it was. NJJ found a garden archaeologist who demonstrated that the offending section had been built in 1933, and planning permission was granted. The garden at East Woodhay was laid out with advice from Mary Keen.

On the first floor, four bedrooms and two bathrooms became six bedrooms and four bathrooms.

PB – "The house was basically a rectangle with a fairly dark, first-floor central area. NJJ solved the problem by designing a magnificent window on the stairs – huge, but totally in character – and putting in a skylight. Together they flooded the landing with light. The skylight was wonderfully weatherproof, too, which shows NJJ wasn't just a pretty face."

NJJ lowered the ceiling in an unworkable passage behind the old dining room to create space above for a long cupboard, accessible from the half-landing. The door, covered with wallpaper, was invisible. Tessa Baring – "It was called the interflora. The grandchildren loved it. All the suitcases and camp beds went in there." PB – "NJJ is a genius at conjuring space from places you wouldn't have imagined; he can't bear to waste it."

Above: The drawing room looking through to the library. NJJ put in double doors between the rooms so that they could be run together for entertaining.

Left: The library. The library and drawing-room bookshelves were designed by NJJ.

Right: A bathroom.

Below: Double-sided sideboard for the kitchen as seen from the dining side.

East Woodhay. Double sided sideboard From dining side

Left: The kitchen interior from the southwest.

Below: The kitchen interior from the northeast. The island, designed by NJJ, is incorporated into the kitchen on one side but is a serving table disguised as a desk on the other.

"The cook had to get down on her knees and push the food through a hatch."

BARTON ABBEY

1995

Robin and Vicky Fleming

Previous page: Barton Abbey's east side, showing the new front door and car park. The Elizabethan stairwell/tower is to the right. The new stairs are to the left of the front door.

Above: Barton Abbey from the south-west.

In 1995, Christopher Gibbs introduced NJJ to Robin and Vicky Fleming, the owners of Barton Abbey. Parts of the house date back to 1570 – when it was probably called Sesswell's Barton Manor House – although the estate's history goes back to Anglo-Saxon times. The house was renamed Barton Abbey by the owner, Henry Hall, in the mid-19th century when the Gothic Revival was in full swing. In 1862, Henry Hall's son, Alexander, employed the architect S.S. Teulon to alter the house. He produced a multi-gabled façade with battlement bay windows and a porch with an oriel window in the Tudor Revival style. The Elizabethan staircase, still winding up its stairwell in well-worn blocks of polished oak, once led to a 92-foot gallery that has long-since disappeared. Barton Abbey's park was one of the last to be created in England.

NJJ – "In the old days, the kitchen wing was up half a level. The cook had to get down on her knees and push the food through a hatch to the butler standing on tiptoe on the other side. We knew that couldn't go on."

The drive, car park and front door were to the south-west of the house. Vicky Fleming was keen for the view down to the lake to be garden and lawn, unobstructed by cars. NJJ – "A bank came pressing down on the back of the house. We gouged it out to make a car park and put the front door on the same side."

The vast stone and pillared hall was decreased in size and turned into a dining room. A gun room was created to the right of the new front door, while the staircase was moved to the right of the new hall. The kitchen was moved to the north side of the dining room and completed by Robert Kime.

Above left: The new hall. An arch from the old hall is visible to the right of the dining room door.

Above right: The gun room.

Left: The dining room. The fireplace is by the 16th-century French sculptor Alain Maynard, who did much of the stonework interior at Longleat. It was sourced by Christopher Gibbs from Leeds Castle where it was being stored.

"We had a beauty parade of architects. One was all Palladio and sweeping staircases."

LOWER LYE

1995

Andrew and Belinda Scott

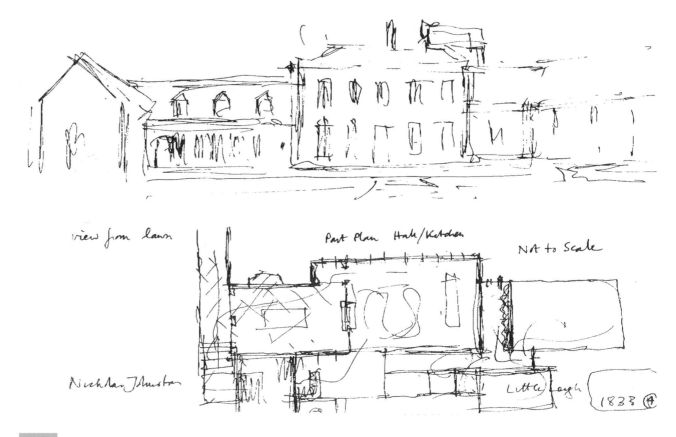

view from lawn

Part Plan Hall/Kitchen

NOT to Scale

Nicholas Johnston

Little Lough

1833

Willie Gething recommended NJJ to Andrew and Belinda Scott, who were about to knock down and rebuild a substantial part of their house in East Knoyle, Wiltshire. Lower Lye's medieval wing is Grade II listed and had been added to in the 1950s.

Belinda Scott – "We had a beauty parade of architects. One was all Palladio and sweeping staircases which wasn't right at all. Nicky always tried to accommodate us but if I was wrong he had a nice way of parking it."

The medieval wing's listed status incurred lengthy deliberations with Salisbury Council's planning and conservation department. BS – "I left the conservation officer to Nicky. His old-fashioned good manners won the day."

NJJ – "We knew we were going to whisk the 1950s additions away and that we'd replace them with the same volume. We had to be sensitive about the height of the new building so it wouldn't dwarf the medieval wing. Fairly soon I thought we'd put the main rooms of the extension into a supposedly 18th-century block and then let the rest trail off to the side like converted outbuildings so that it wouldn't have too much dominance over the existing."

The new wing contains the nucleus for living: a large kitchen, a children's room and the backstairs to the bedrooms. The medieval wing houses the low-ceilinged, ancient-beamed drawing room with a bedroom and bathroom above it.

NJJ – "The site was rather awkward but very interesting. You come down a steep, grassy

Left: The height of the addition roof is slightly lower than the sketch.

Below: A view of the new entrance and hall (to the right) joining the existing medieval wing.

hill to a house nestling into the landscape with uninterrupted views to Alfred's Tower. In order to avoid digging out monstrous chunks of hill, the new hall had to be half a level above the ground floor of the rest of the house, tying the layers of the house together."

The stone hall has two staircases, one twisting upwards to the right of the front door and another to the left, leading down a half-flight to a corridor with three arches into the dining room on the right. Above and to the left of the corner fireplace, a round opening gives onto a top-lit upper passage, bringing an unexpected shaft of brightness to the north-facing hall.

BS – "Nicky was a delight to work with. He only put his foot down once, in the nicest possible way, about French windows. He said absolutely not."

NJJ – "No, I couldn't let her have French windows. The sash opening with small doors underneath is perfect for a house on that scale. It's the sort of thing they have at Hampton Court. I'm glad I won."

BS – "It's odd – there was a bit of sniffiness when we decided to build a new house, but everyone wants to do it now."

Above left: The hall.

Above right: Arches through to the dining room from the corridor.

"He liked the idea of rowing across the lake to a hideaway cottage."

COTTAGE ORNÉE

1995

Prince Bandar

In 1992, JCA had taken on the considerable task of modernising and extending Glympton for Prince Bandar of Saudi Arabia.

NJJ – "In 1995, we were asked to design a little house – a sort of Petit Trianon. Prince Bandar wanted somewhere peaceful, away from the bustle of the main house. He liked the idea of rowing across the lake to a hideaway cottage.

"The requirements were, on the face of it, quite simple. A nice big sitting room with a galleried bedroom, a big bathroom, a hobby kitchen (the sort where someone brings something through and you pretend you cooked it yourself) but the infrastructure was enormous. The huge basement,

completely out of sight, included a room for the bodyguards, another kitchen for the staff, boilers, air conditioners, a machinery room and security facilities. It was modelled on Blaize Hamlet, a collection of 12 lovely cottages designed by Nash on the outskirts of Bristol, some with steep roofs, some thatched. We got permission for a new house on a greenfield site because Dr John Martin Robinson – the archivist at Arundel for a time, and a great architectural historian and guru – wrote us a paper for the planning application in support of the cottage which I thought was bound to get everyone's backs up. The theme was that any gentleman's park of this size would have had a Cottage Ornée and it was only by an oversight that there wasn't one, and they swallowed it!"

GLYMPTON
PARK PAVILION

VIEW FROM LAKE.

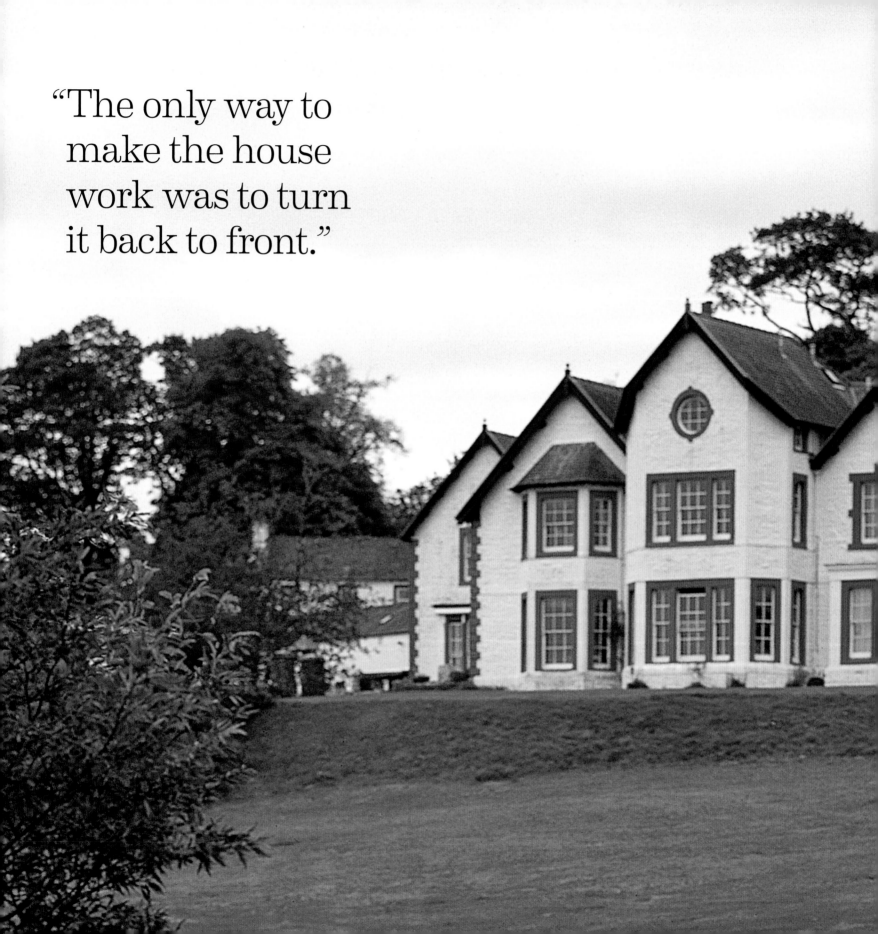

"The only way to make the house work was to turn it back to front."

CROCHMORE

1997

Ben and Silvy Weatherall

rochmore sits on the side of a hill, with far-reaching views looking south towards Criffel and the Solway Firth in Dumfries and Galloway. Ben and Silvy Weatherall (NJJ's daughter), returning from five years abroad, were keen to crack on with much-needed changes to their large Victorian farmhouse.

Silvy Weatherall – "Dad suggested that we lived in the house for a year before starting any work so we could log our needs over the changing seasons. Shooting parties, fishing, golfing, rain and a growing family flagged up a large kitchen, boot room and cellar as top priorities."

The house, built on bedrock in 1896, was designed for living with domestic staff. The small kitchen was at the back of the house – a long walk from the dining room. The central, double-height hall commanded the best views.

NJJ – "The only way to make the house work was to turn it back to front and put the kitchen in the hall. The front door was on the south side so when you opened it a gale blew in. We moved the entrance from the south to the sheltered north side of the house, clearing parked cars from the views. What is now the hall was a long, dark passage with storerooms leading off it. At the far end was the drawing room, added in the 1960s."

Opening up the back half of the house made the awkward drawing-room extension more central to the house. The room had an odd, L-shaped kink – it became a walk-in drinks cupboard leading on to an insulated, ground-floor cellar.

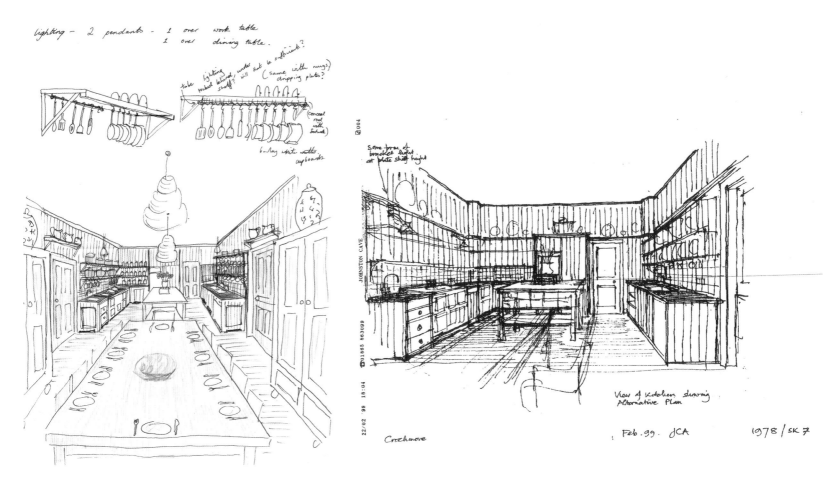

lighting – 2 pendants – 1 over work table
1 over dining table.

SW – "He talked us through the whole process, down to drawing the cross-section of a cornice. When we came to think about ideas for the kitchen, we both drew our ideas with plans and elevation drawings and faxed them through to each other. Client and architect came up with pretty much the same scheme. He knew what we wanted."

The building work was realised by Waughs of Dumfries.

Above left: Silvy Weatherall's sketch sent to NJJ. He sent her one at the same time that was almost identical.

Above right: NJJ's near-identical sketch of the kitchen.

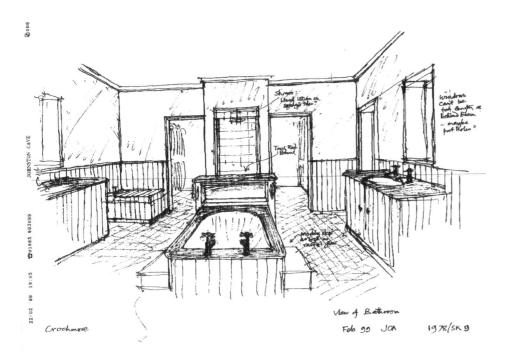

View of Bathroom
Feb 99 JCA   1978/SK 9

Crochmore

Above: One of the bathrooms.

*Opposite page: The hall, with
banisters designed by NJJ.*

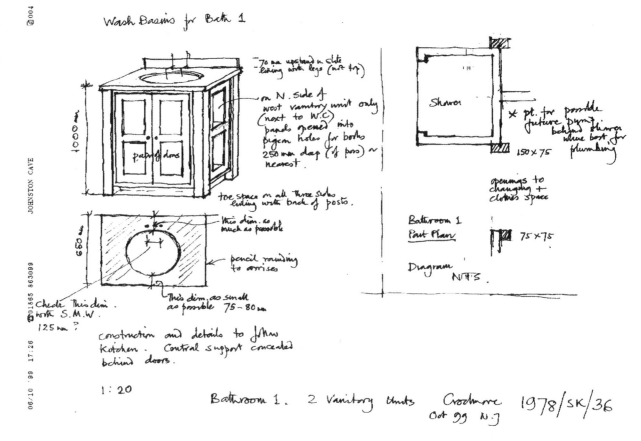

Wash Basins for Bath 1

1:20

Bathroom 1.   2 Vanitory Units   Crochmore   1978/SK/36
                Oct 99 NJ

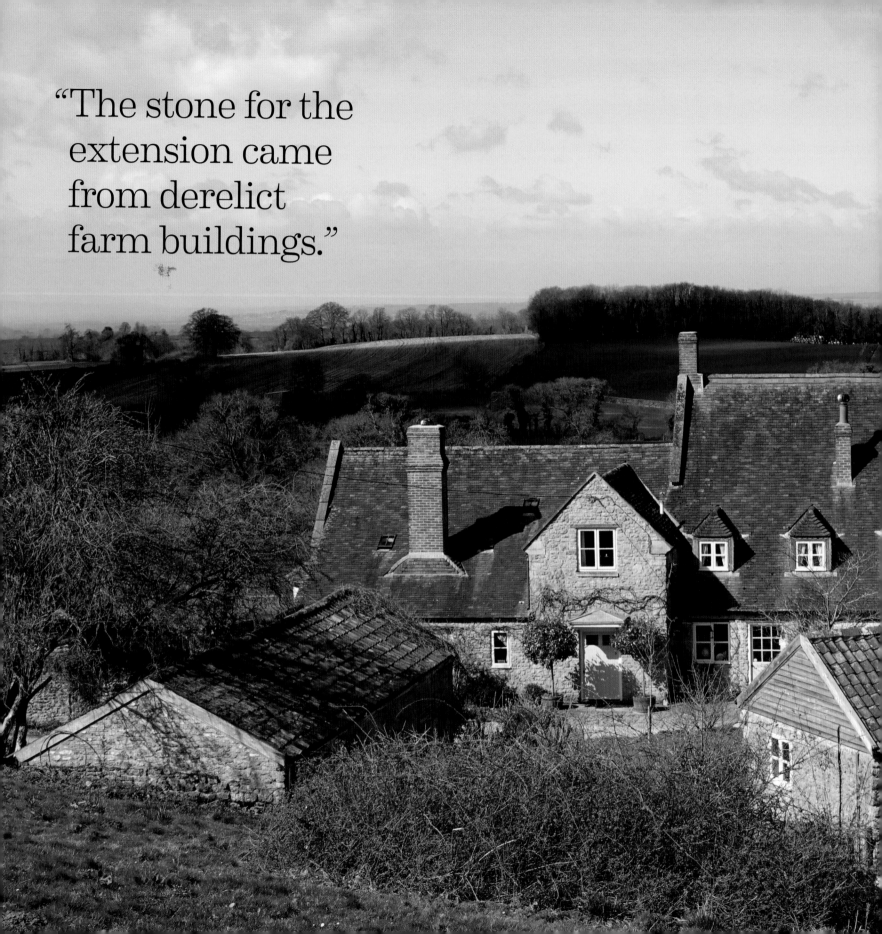

"The stone for the extension came from derelict farm buildings."

NEW PARK FARM

1998

Charlie and Amanda Ellingworth

The plan for New Park Farm was to extend the 17th-century farmhouse on the southeast side. The new wing was to include a hall, staircase, two bedrooms, a bathroom and a large room on the ground floor.

Amanda Ellingworth – "NJJ was sketching ideas on the back of an envelope. He asked us what the room was to be used for. We replied that, as it was to be south-facing, we would like it to be for our three boys who were then seven, five and two. He paused, put down his fork and said, 'In ten years time your children will get up at midday, stagger downstairs, draw the curtains, watch TV until it's dark, and then go to the pub. Do you really want them to have the sunniest room in the house?'. It became the drawing room."

Above: The south side.

Below: The drawing room window.

The stone for the extension came from derelict farm buildings on the Ellingworths' farm and others nearby. The stone for all the buildings would have been sourced from the same quarry, hence the seamless match between old and new.

The drive to New Park Farm approaches from the north down a steep hill. Cars are parked on a ledge, leaving an open area of garden in front of the house.

Above left: The new roof and chimney.

Top: The drawing room from the southeast.

Above: The new hall and staircase. Behind the bookshelf on the right is the party wall with the old farm.

"I saw a beautiful staircase that had been turned into a box room."

COWHILL

2003

Percy and Clara Weatherall

View of House from the South
Proposed new wing on extreme left.

View of Proposed Courtyard
Looking north west.

Above left: A sketch of Cowhill from the south side, showing the proposed addition at the left rear.

Above right: A view of the proposed courtyard looking north-west.

Opposite page: Cowhill from the north side, showing the new extension.

In 1899, Henry Keswick married a Miss Johnston of Cowhill (distantly related to NJJ). With her came a Victorian pile, its Georgian original buried in a series of enlargements. Henry Keswick added a baronial tower to the east side.

Henry's son David inherited Cowhill. In 1942, a chimney fire ran out of control and destroyed two-thirds of the house. Italian prisoners of war billeted there were ordered to save the chattels, including the contents of the wine cellar.

Percy Weatherall – "For ten days the Italians were discovered in ditches surrounded by empty magnums of first-growth claret. The fire never did get to the cellar."

David Keswick's intention to rebuild Cowhill was hampered by post-war planning restrictions and rationing of materials. Eventually, he and his architect, W.A.S. Lloyd, retained the tower and restored part of the adjoining ruins on a much reduced scale. A second, less serious fire in 1972 gave an opportunity for minor improvements to the previous restoration. David Keswick's daughter Sophy and her husband, Captain Anthony Weatherall, moved into Cowhill in 1976.

PW – "In 2000 my parents, in the foothills of old age, decided to move into the stables. Clara (NJJ's daughter) and I were living in Hong Kong but a return to Cowhill was in prospect. The house clearly needed a 50-year service and we didn't have to look far for an architect. Clara, Nicky and I had great fun

Top: The new slate passage.

Bottom left: Cowhill staircase.

Bottom right: The dining room. NJJ – "The ceiling was Percy's idea. I was a bit worried about the gold, but I've become accustomed to it now."

Opposite page, top: The kitchen.

Opposite page, bottom: The pantry.

considering our options. The plans were worked and reworked for two years before Nicky made it clear to us that the only sensible way to proceed was to build on."

The extension included a dining room, kitchen and pantry within walking distance of each other. Two bedrooms that were lost in the renovations of the main house were replaced in the new build. Dark spaces were opened up and a passage made between old and new.

NJJ – "I'd visited Cowhill before Clara and Percy took it over. There were tiny spiral stairs that went straight into the drawing room, or you went through catacombs to find the stairs into the old part of the house. I peeped behind a curtain and saw a beautiful staircase that had been turned into a box room. I thought it should be revived. The hall had lost its shape – it was used as a sitting room after the fire because of all the water damage. We put it back to its original which leads you towards the foot of the staircase."

PW – "Being married to the architect's daughter threw up one or two bouncers but overall it was an exciting and wholly agreeable experience."

Work kicked off in early 2003 and was broadly complete by 2005.

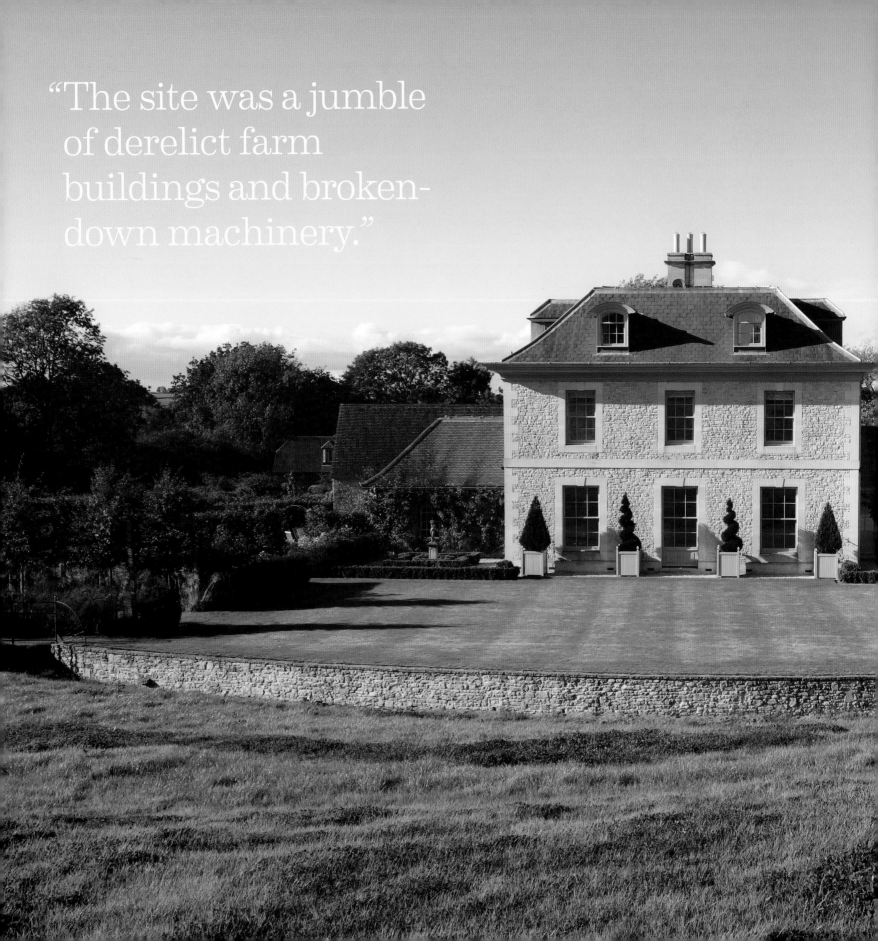

"The site was a jumble of derelict farm buildings and broken-down machinery."

HOLLAND
FARM

2006

Willie and Nickie Gething

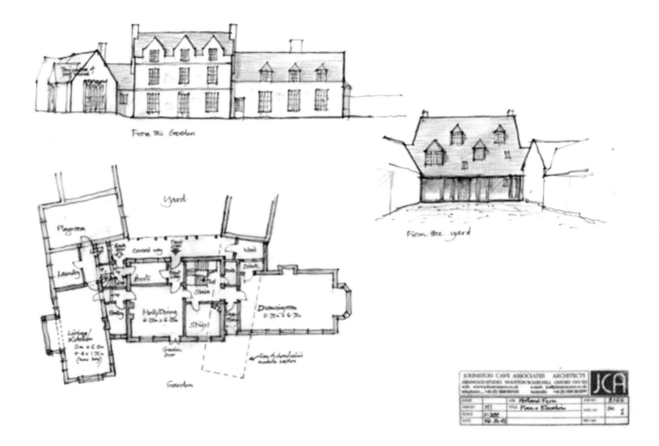

Right: The first sketches for Holland Farm show three storeys with a cat-slide roof, reminiscent of Lutyens.

Willie Gething always wanted to live in Somerset, but when he and his wife Nickie started looking for a house "they were either huge like Maiden Bradley or farmhouses with six-foot ceilings that I couldn't stand up in."

In 2002 they bought an idyllic plot at the foot of a grassy knoll looking up to Alfred's Tower. The site was a jumble of derelict farm buildings and broken-down machinery, with a dilapidated Dutch barn and a small 19th-century house. The Gethings decided to start from scratch and spent the next three years working out the plans for what would become Holland Farm. "We didn't care how long it took to get the drawings right," says Willie. "We interviewed five architects but Nicky was the one who listened very carefully to us. He wanted to understand how we lived then, and how we'd be living in ten years

time before he started sketching. He designed from the inside out, not the other way around."

NJJ used the layout and angles of the existing farm buildings to create roughly symmetrical wings for the classically proportioned centre block of the house.

For the east wing, a study replaced the pig barn and the pony stable became a playroom. The wing also has two spare bedrooms and bathrooms. A spectacular kitchen with a new oak roof and ceiling-height, arched windows replaces the barn. The barrel-vaulted dining room stands on the footprint of the old cow sheds, creating an intriguingly angled hub between the drawing room, kitchen and stairs. NJJ's schemes were realised by Mouldings of Salisbury.

Left: A sketch overlay with consideration for specific furniture. The east side of the house is still proposed as two storeys.

Middle: A rough sketch showing the main house with wings inspired by the original outbuildings.

Below: The classically proportioned, slate-roofed main house lies between the footprints of the demolished farm buildings. The fine-cut stone came from a local quarry. Rougher-cut stone was used for the wings. The varied roof tiling is based on the original outbuildings.

*Above: Holland Farm before
and after photos from the
western side of the house.*

Above: The kitchen and dining room from the west.

Left: Looking through the arch to the east side.

Right: The kitchen's west-facing window.

Left: Looking from the back door passage through the kitchen to the dining room.

Below: The drawing room faces south with a view of the banks up to Alfred's Tower. The tall windows were initially a sticking point for local planners.

Opposite page: The kitchen's west-facing window.

Above left: The kitchen's east-facing window.

Above right: The dining room.

Left: Looking through the hall from the left of the stairs to the passage beyond.

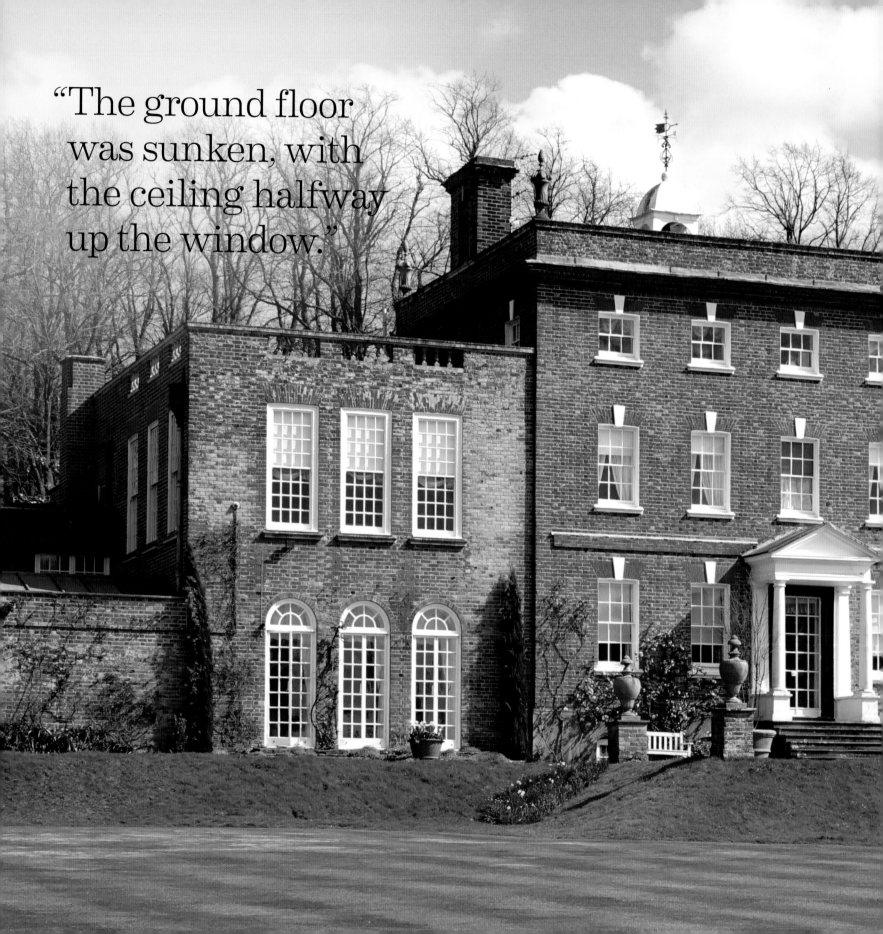

"The ground floor was sunken, with the ceiling halfway up the window."

OARE
HOUSE   2007

Henry and Tessa Keswick

Above: Oare House, west elevation.

Above right: A rainwater hopper with Henry and Tessa Keswick's initials. The brickwork is by Symm and Co.

Oare House was built in around 1740 for a London wine merchant. Formal gardens, a large plantation and a summer house spoke of prosperity and grandeur. The estate declined in the 19th century, however, and was gradually sold off. Sir Geoffrey Fry bought Oare in 1921 and commissioned Clough Williams-Ellis to renovate the house and estate cottages.

Williams-Ellis remodelled the drawing room, extending it with an even bigger library and a bedroom above. He mirrored the façade by putting an equivalent on the north side (facing west) but simply stuck it over what was there without altering the floor levels to work with the exterior.

Tessa Keswick – "The house was a complete jumble. The floor for the new dining room had to be raised three feet."

NJJ – "Before we put the dining room on the same level as the kitchen, you had to drag the food upstairs. The ground-floor room was sunken, a sort of semi-basement, with the ceiling halfway up the window. In the same way, the windowsills in the first-floor bedroom were nearer the ceiling than the floor."

Oare's Grade I listing required the highest level of help from English Heritage when applying for planning permission. NJJ – "There were problems, but English Heritage saw the point in trying to make

the house work. There was a chimney we thought they might baulk at us removing, but they didn't."

The kitchen, pantry and laundry room were built to the north side of the new dining room, behind the garden wall that extends from the west-facing façade. Permission to raise the height of the wall to hide the new build behind involved lengthy negotiations. The old kitchen is now a nursery.

Henry Keswick – "JCA revolutionised the house. We were here for about 20 years before we had the work done – we were desperate to do it but it was so expensive, I had to save up."

Above left: Various interiors including the dining room and first floor bedroom in the north wing.

Top: The dining room. The pink-marble pillar and mirrored interior was designed by John Stefanidis. Tessa Keswick – "Clough Williams-Ellis was very theatrical. We wanted the interiors to reflect that."

Above: The first floor bedroom. Interior design by John Stefanidis.

A MODEST MISCELLANY

Bookcase Screening WC

Right: Shelves to separate the lavatory from the bath at Rotten Row House.

NJJ – "I rather love designing furniture. In 1967 I put a cupboard either side of the window seat for Gillian Fane at Chantry Cottage. I've done that two or three times, it makes rather a nice wall. When Gillian and Julian [Fane] moved to Rotten Row House in 1985, they had so many books, we had to find all sorts of places for them. We made a bookshelf in the bathroom that screened the lav from the bath, and the landing when the door was open. The landing door has changed now. We made shelves around doors and under windows. Everywhere we could, really."

Landing ~~Bookshelves~~ Bookshelves

Eccleston Square
Dining Room

Cupboards +
window seat

*Above: sketches for shelves,
a dining room door and
cupboards for Gillian Fane
(Eccleston Square, Chantry
Cottage and Rotten Row
House).*

*Top, left to right: Shelves
surrounding the door between
the front and back halls;
dining room shelves at*

*Rotten Row House; window
shutters to match the
cupboard (shown previous
page) in the spare room.*

Above and opposite: The swimming pool pavilion at Sparshot, built in 1986 for Adrian and Judy Swire.

NJJ – "It was Judy's idea for the changing rooms to be in the manner of a cricket pavilion."

Printed in China

First Printing, 2015

ISBN 978-0-9933240-0-0

Cowhill Tower
Holywood
Dumfries
DG2 0TR

Orangery

Looking N.E. - Garden

Bank Dropping to South.

The entrance front from the main approach.

Looking N.W. Garden Front